INTRODUCING
ISSUES WITH
OPPOSING
VIEWPOINTS®

# Health Care

Noël Merino, *Book Editor*

**GREENHAVEN PRESS**
*A part of Gale, Cengage Learning*

GALE
CENGAGE Learning™

Detroit • New York • San Francisco • New Haven, Conn • Waterville, Maine • London

GALE
CENGAGE Learning™

Christine Nasso, *Publisher*
Elizabeth Des Chenes, *Managing Editor*

© 2010 Greenhaven Press, a part of Gale, Cengage Learning

Gale and Greenhaven Press are registered trademarks used herein under license.

*For more information, contact:*
Greenhaven Press
27500 Drake Rd.
Farmington Hills, MI 48331-3535
Or you can visit our Internet site at gale.cengage.com

Articles in Greenhaven Press anthologies are often edited for length to meet page requirements. In addition, original titles of these works are changed to clearly present the main thesis and to explicitly indicate the author's opinion. Every effort is made to ensure that Greenhaven Press accurately reflects the original intent of the authors. Every effort has been made to trace the owners of copyrighted material.

Cover image copyright © Andrew Geutry, 2009. Used under license from Shutterstock.com.

**LIBRARY OF CONGRESS CATALOGING-IN-PUBLICATION DATA**

Health care / Noël Merino, book editor.
    p. cm. -- (Introducing issues with opposing viewpoints)
  Includes bibliographical references and index.
  ISBN 978-0-7377-4477-4 (hardcover)
  1. Medical care--United States. I. Merino, Noël.
  RA395.A3H3856 2009
  362.10973--dc22
                             2009025867

Printed in the United States of America
1 2 3 4 5 6 7 13 12 11 10 09

# Contents

# Foreword

Indulging in a wide spectrum of ideas, beliefs, and perspectives is a critical cornerstone of democracy. After all, it is often debates over differences of opinion, such as whether to legalize abortion, how to treat prisoners, or when to enact the death penalty, that shape our society and drive it forward. Such diversity of thought is frequently regarded as the hallmark of a healthy and civilized culture. As the Reverend Clifford Schutjer of the First Congregational Church in Mansfield, Ohio, declared in a 2001 sermon, "Surrounding oneself with only like-minded people, restricting what we listen to or read only to what we find agreeable is irresponsible. Refusing to entertain doubts once we make up our minds is a subtle but deadly form of arrogance." With this advice in mind, Introducing Issues with Opposing Viewpoints books aim to open readers' minds to the critically divergent views that comprise our world's most important debates.

Introducing Issues with Opposing Viewpoints simplifies for students the enormous and often overwhelming mass of material now available via print and electronic media. Collected in every volume is an array of opinions that captures the essence of a particular controversy or topic. Introducing Issues with Opposing Viewpoints books embody the spirit of nineteenth-century journalist Charles A. Dana's axiom: "Fight for your opinions, but do not believe that they contain the whole truth, or the only truth." Absorbing such contrasting opinions teaches students to analyze the strength of an argument and compare it to its opposition. From this process readers can inform and strengthen their own opinions, or be exposed to new information that will change their minds. Introducing Issues with Opposing Viewpoints is a mosaic of different voices. The authors are statesmen, pundits, academics, journalists, corporations, and ordinary people who have felt compelled to share their experiences and ideas in a public forum. Their words have been collected from newspapers, journals, books, speeches, interviews, and the Internet, the fastest growing body of opinionated material in the world.

Introducing Issues with Opposing Viewpoints shares many of the well-known features of its critically acclaimed parent series, Opposing Viewpoints. The articles are presented in a pro/con format, allowing readers to absorb divergent perspectives side by side. Active reading questions preface each viewpoint, requiring the student to approach the material thoughtfully and carefully. Useful charts, graphs, and cartoons supplement each article. A thorough introduction provides readers with crucial background on an issue. An annotated bibliography points the reader toward articles, books, and Web sites that contain additional information on the topic. An appendix of organizations to contact contains a wide variety of charities, nonprofit organizations, political groups, and private enterprises that each hold a position on the issue at hand. Finally, a comprehensive index allows readers to locate content quickly and efficiently.

Introducing Issues with Opposing Viewpoints is also significantly different from Opposing Viewpoints. As the series title implies, its presentation will help introduce students to the concept of opposing viewpoints and learn to use this material to aid in critical writing and debate. The series' four-color, accessible format makes the books attractive and inviting to readers of all levels. In addition, each viewpoint has been carefully edited to maximize a reader's understanding of the content. Short but thorough viewpoints capture the essence of an argument. A substantial, thought-provoking essay question placed at the end of each viewpoint asks the student to further investigate the issues raised in the viewpoint, compare and contrast two authors' arguments, or consider how one might go about forming an opinion on the topic at hand. Each viewpoint contains sidebars that include at-a-glance information and handy statistics. A Facts About section located in the back of the book further supplies students with relevant facts and figures.

Following in the tradition of the Opposing Viewpoints series, Greenhaven Press continues to provide readers with invaluable exposure to the controversial issues that shape our world. As John Stuart Mill once wrote: "The only way in which a human being can make some approach to knowing the whole of a subject is by hearing what can be said about it by persons of every variety of opinion and studying all modes in which it can be looked at by every character of mind. No wise man ever acquired his wisdom in any mode but this." It is to this principle that Introducing Issues with Opposing Viewpoints books are dedicated.

# Introduction

*"While this bill is short of our ultimate goal of health reform, it is a down payment, and is an essential start."*

—Henry A. Waxman, House of Representatives, Democrat, California

*"We've watched as SCHIP has been slowly replacing employer health plans with government-paid health plans with spiraling costs to taxpayers."*

—Tom McClintock, House of Representatives, Republican, California

Although the best way to provide health care to Americans is a matter of much debate—whether through a government-sponsored single-payer system, a consumer-driven private insurance system, or some other option—no one disputes that a growing number of Americans go without health insurance. The U.S. Census Bureau found that in 2007, 15 percent of the population, over 45 million people, did not have health insurance. Among these millions of uninsured were over 8 million children under eighteen years old. The State Children's Health Insurance Program (SCHIP) is a U.S. federal government program that was created in 1997 to help expand health insurance coverage for children. Nonetheless, the program has not been without controversy, most recently due to President Barack Obama's expansion of the program in February 2009.

The original legislation for SCHIP was sponsored by Senator Ted Kennedy, Democrat from Massachusetts, and Senator Orrin Hatch, Republican from Utah, and passed during the Clinton administration as part of the Balanced Budget Act of 1997. As with Medicaid, SCHIP is jointly administered by federal and state governments. The federal Centers for Medicare and Medicaid Services (CMS) sets requirements for the SCHIP program, but within these requirements the states are free to run the programs as they see fit. Some states use the SCHIP funds to expand Medicaid, and others run separate child health programs. Prior to the passage of SCHIP, children without health insurance had to rely on Medicaid or state-sponsored health insurance programs. Eligibility for Medicaid is set by federal and state law. One of the goals of SCHIP was to help to provide health insurance for children whose families did not qualify for Medicaid but nonetheless could not afford health insurance—most states have set the eligibility for SCHIP at 200 percent of the federal poverty level.

According to the Congressional Budget Office's (CBO) analysis, "among children living in families with income between 100 percent and 200 percent of the poverty level (the group with the greatest increase in eligibility for public coverage under SCHIP), the uninsurance rate fell from 22.5 percent in 1996 (the year before SCHIP was enacted) to 16.9 percent in 2005, a reduction of 25 percent." CBO notes, however, that not all who enroll in SCHIP represent further coverage extant to the uninsured—this is because some people who enroll in SCHIP choose it over private coverage they would have bought without SCHIP. CBO estimates that "for every 100 children who enroll as a result of SCHIP, there is a corresponding reduction in private coverage of between 25 and 50 children."

In 2007 both houses of Congress passed a bill (HR 976) to expand coverage of SCHIP, but President George W. Bush vetoed the bill, citing a concern that Congress was trying to "federalize health care." This bill included coverage for pregnant women and illegal immigrant children. A second bill (HR 3963) passed both houses of Congress later in the year—this time barring all adults and children of illegal immigrants from coverage—but Bush also vetoed this bill, telling Congress that the bill "moves our country's health care system in the wrong direction." After the election of Obama, in January 2009 both houses of Congress passed a bill (HR 2) that expanded health coverage to 4 million more children and was signed into law by Obama on February 4, 2009. The bill allows states the option to cover pregnant women (citizens or legal immigrants) and the children of legal immigrants without the previously mandated five-year waiting period for legal immigrants.

The debate about SCHIP illustrates the central debates about how to address the problem of the uninsured. Bush had opposed the Democratic proposals to expand SCHIP from the beginning, citing his concern in early 2007 prior to his two vetoes: "Their goal is to take incremental steps down the path to government-run health care for every American." Bush worried that "Government-run health care would deprive Americans of the choice and competition that comes from the private market." Citing a common view among Republicans, Bush argued that the correct solution to the problem of the uninsured in America is to "work to make basic private health insurance affordable for all Americans." During debate about the 2009 expansion of SCHIP in the Senate, Republican senator from Arizona John McCain told Obama, "Some of us who look at this may view it as another effort to eliminate, over time, private insurance in America, and I am concerned about that."

On the other side of the debate are those who see SCHIP as one important part of ensuring that all Americans have access to health care. During debate of SCHIP in the Senate, Democratic senator from New Jersey Robert Menendez commented on the public health interest of SCHIP:

> Children, whether they be in a classroom or on a playground, are contagious. So whether it is a legal immigrant child or a U.S.-born citizen, the bottom line is they are playing in that playground together, sitting in the classroom together. If one has health care and the other doesn't because we have an arbitrary bar, it is easy to get some cold or disease that is contagious, so there is a public health interest for all of us.

Upon the passage of SCHIP in the Senate, President Obama stated, "Providing health care to more than ten million children through the Children's Health Insurance Program will serve as a down payment on my commitment to ensure that every American has access to quality, affordable health care."

As in the case of the debate about SCHIP, the debate about health care in the United States revolves around the issues of the proper role of government involvement, the proper role of private insurance, and the viability of proposals for health care reform. These issues, as well as other issues about the state of the health care system in the United States, are explored in *Introducing Issues with Opposing Viewpoints: Health Care.*

# Chapter 1

# What Is the Current State of the Health Care System in America?

*The state of health care in America is a subject of continuing controversy.*

# The U.S. Health Care System Offers the Best Health Care in the World

*"If you are diagnosed with a serious illness, the United States is where you want to receive treatment."*

**Michael D. Tanner**

In the following viewpoint Michael D. Tanner contends that American health care is the best in the world. Drawing on his own experience with prostate cancer, Tanner contends that treatment options of the sort he experienced, coupled with the reputation of American medical treatment centers and researchers, make the United States the best place in the world for health care. Tanner is a senior fellow at the Cato Institute, where he heads research into a variety of domestic policies with a particular emphasis on health care reform. He is coauthor, along with Michael F. Cannon, of *Healthy Competition: What's Holding Back Health Care and How to Free It.*

**AS YOU READ, CONSIDER THE FOLLOWING QUESTIONS:**
1. According to Tanner, how many American men will die from prostate cancer?
2. What percentage of British prostate cancer patients never get to see an oncologist, or cancer doctor?
3. According to Tanner, Americans played a key role in what percentage of the most important medical advances in the last thirty years?

Twenty years of public policy research on health care recently came home to me in a very personal way when I was diagnosed with prostate cancer.

Because I live in a country with a free-market health-care system, I had a choice of treatments: surgery, external radiation, brachytherapy. I was able to find the doctor and hospital I felt most comfortable with. As a result, I can expect to live a long, healthy, cancer-free life.

If I lived elsewhere, this might not have been the outcome.

In most countries with national health insurance, the preferred treatment for prostate cancer is . . . to do nothing.

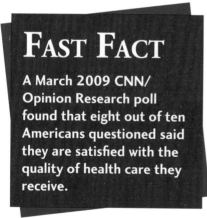

**FAST FACT**

A March 2009 CNN/Opinion Research poll found that eight out of ten Americans questioned said they are satisfied with the quality of health care they receive.

Prostate cancer is a slow-moving disease. Most patients are older and will live several years after diagnosis. So it is not cost-effective under socialized medicine to treat the disease too aggressively. This saves money, but at a more human cost.

Though American men are more likely to be diagnosed with prostate cancer than their counterparts in other countries, we are less likely to die from the disease. Less than 1 in 5 American men with prostate cancer will die from it, but 57 percent of British men and nearly half of French and German men will. Even in Canada, a quarter of men diagnosed with prostate cancer die from the disease.

The one common characteristic of all national health-care systems is that they ration care. Sometimes they ration it explicitly, denying certain types of treatment altogether. More often, they ration more indirectly, imposing global budgets or other cost constraints that limit availability of high-tech medical equipment or impose long waits for treatments.

Consider this: 7 in 10 Canadian provinces report sending prostate cancer patients to the United States for radiation treatment. In Great Britain, roughly 40 percent of cancer patients never get to see an oncologist.

There are problems with the American health-care system. Too many Americans lack health insurance and/or are unable to afford the type of care I received. We need to do more to lower health-care costs and increase access. Both patients and providers need better and more useful information.

The system is riddled with waste and the quality uneven. Government health-care programs like Medicare and Medicaid threaten future generations with enormous debt and taxes.

*A patient consults with his physician about his prostate cancer therapy. The author argues that American health care is superior to all other countries' and points to statistics of prostate cancer survival rates as evidence.*

# Incidence and Mortality of Prostate Cancer

## Incidence

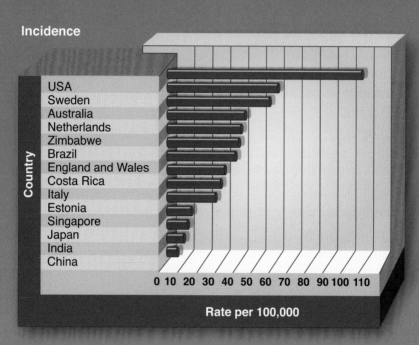

## Mortality

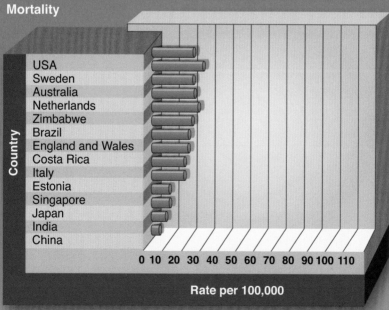

Taken from: M. Quinn and P. Babb, "Patterns and Trends in Prostate Cancer Incidence, Survival, Prevalence, and Mortality," *BJU International*, vol. 90, 2002.

Yet we should never forget that America offers the world's highest-quality health care. Most of the world's top doctors, hospitals and research facilities are in the United States. Eighteen of the last 25 winners of the Nobel Prize in Medicine either are U.S. citizens or work here. Half of all the major new medicines introduced worldwide in the last 20 years were developed by U.S. companies. Americans played a key role in 80 percent of the most important medical advances of the last 30 years. By almost any measure, if you are diagnosed with a serious illness, the United States is where you want to receive treatment. That is why tens of thousands of patients from around the world come here every year.

The guiding principle of health-care reform should be the Hippocratic admonition, "First do no harm." Those calling for national health care in America would destroy the things that make American health care so good. More regulation, subsidies and control would simply drain the medical market of the quality, dynamism and innovation that saves lives.

What American health care needs is more choice and competition, not less. We've started down that route through Health Savings Accounts and other market-oriented reforms, but more needs to be done. My Cato colleague, Michael Cannon, and I recently published a new book, "Healthy Competition: What's Holding Back American Health Care and How to Free It," outlining comprehensive market-oriented reforms that would make health care more affordable, expand consumer choice, and preserve the quality of care. We hope it will serve as a starting point in the political debate to come.

But, for now, I for one say, God bless American health care.

**EVALUATING THE AUTHOR'S ARGUMENTS:**

In this viewpoint Tanner contends that U.S. health care is the best in the world, while admitting that it has some problems. What are some of the problems he identifies?

# The U.S. Health Care System Is Not Working

*"The U.S. now ranks 19th out of a group of 19 major industrialized countries on an important measure of health system performance."*

**Karen Davis**

In the following viewpoint Karen Davis argues that the U.S. health care system is broken. Davis maintains that numerous people are experiencing financial problems related to health care, exacerbating the U.S. economic crisis. She claims that access to health care is a huge problem, with large numbers of people lacking access to affordable care. Davis believes that reform is possible but will need to involve changes to a variety of components of the health care system. Karen Davis is president of the Commonwealth Fund, a private foundation that aims to promote a high-performing health care system that achieves better access, improved quality, and greater efficiency.

AS YOU READ, CONSIDER THE FOLLOWING QUESTIONS:
1. What fraction of American adults under the age of sixty-five report being uninsured or underinsured, forgoing needed care, or struggling to pay medical bills or debt, according to Davis?
2. The author agrees with President Barack Obama that health care reform is integral to what?

Karen Davis, "You Can Get There from Here: Mapping the Way to a Transformed U.S. Health System," The Commonwealth Fund, January 2009. Reproduced by permission.

3. Davis argues that the system of paying health care providers needs to be reworked to correct the imbalance in payment between what two kinds of care?

I n a speech he gave nearly half a century ago, John F. Kennedy noted that the Chinese symbol for crisis comprises the characters representing both danger and opportunity. Today, his observation could not be more relevant. The potent combination of recent events in the United States has presented the nation's leaders with a historic opportunity to fix our broken health care system.

## A Health Care Crisis

With 116 million adults under age 65 reporting health care–related financial issues, the nation's health care crisis and economic crisis have become inextricably intertwined. As unemployment grows, more Americans will join the ranks of the uninsured. States under pressure to balance their budgets are already making cuts in health programs that serve low-income adults and children. Already families—even those with insurance—are struggling to pay their share of premiums and medical expenses. Two-thirds of all adults under age 65 report being uninsured or underinsured, forgoing needed care, or struggling to pay medical bills or accumulated medical debt.

Ours is the only industrialized nation that fails to ensure that all its citizens have access to affordable health care. We are slipping further behind what other countries achieve with their more modest investment in health care: the U.S. now ranks 19th out of a group of 19 major industrialized countries on an important measure of health system performance: mortality amenable to medical care. If we did as well as the best-performing countries, we would have 100,000 fewer deaths each year.

Access is not the only problem. The poor performance of the U.S. health system also adds to the economic crisis. Currently, the United States spends twice as much per person as other major industrialized countries, saddling American businesses—especially those with aging workforces—with high expenses. It adds to burdens on taxpayers and squeezes other public priority needs, from education to the nation's aging infrastructure.

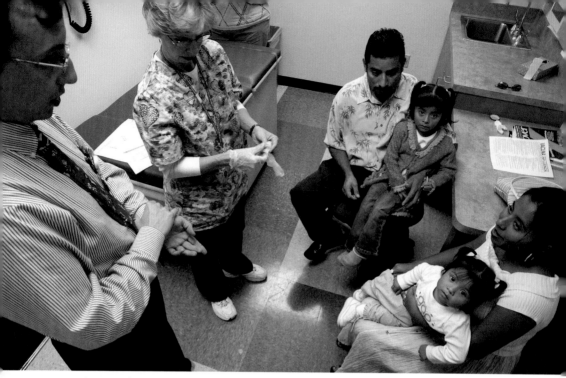

*In the United States nearly two-thirds of adults under sixty-five are underinsured or uninsured.*

## An Opening for Change

President Barack Obama has noted, rightly, that health care reform is integral to economic recovery. Investing now in the information technology and other tools needed to modernize our health system, as well as in children's health that will contribute to a healthy workforce in the future, will pay dividends in lower costs and greater productivity in the future.

As we have seen so recently in response to the financial crisis, when government and the business community work together they can creatively address urgent national needs. Reform of our health care system is such a need. Government, business, purchasers, providers, patients—each must be part of the solution. We must all be willing to change—and to put what is in the best interest of patients first—if we want to reap the rewards of a high-value, equitable health care system.

We are fortunate that within our imperfect health care system are examples of all the components that, properly organized, reformed, and financed, can enable the nation to provide high-quality, affordable care to virtually every American. Systematically applying and disseminating what we know works would help put the U.S. on the path to a high-performance health system.

As a nation, we stand today at the threshold of an era ripe with opportunity. A new administration in Washington—one that has promised serious attention to health care reform—gives us hope that providing insurance to all Americans, reducing costs, and improving quality and equity will all soon be in the forefront of our national policy debate.

## A High Performance Health System

The Commonwealth Fund Commission on a High Performance Health System has issued a call to action for health reform. It underscores that a critical step toward achieving a high performance health system is to provide insurance coverage to all Americans. But equally essential are bold actions that simultaneously improve the quality and efficiency of health care delivery—so that we improve the lives of Americans, alter the trajectory of health care costs, and make it easier for patients to obtain the care they need and providers to practice the best of modern medicine.

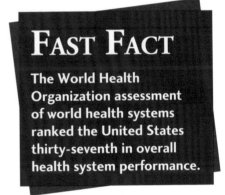

**FAST FACT**

The World Health Organization assessment of world health systems ranked the United States thirty-seventh in overall health system performance.

The Commission calls for the following steps to be taken:

*Provide affordable health coverage for all.* It is time that all Americans received the security of health care coverage enjoyed by citizens of every other major industrialized country. Providing everyone—regardless of age or employment status—with affordable insurance options, including a comprehensive package of benefits, will enhance access to care. This, in turn, will help reduce disparities in care, increase the proportion of people receiving appropriate primary care to prevent illness, and improve the care and health of millions of Americans living with chronic conditions.

*Reform provider payment.* Our open-ended fee-for-service payment system must be overhauled to reduce wasteful and ineffective care and to spur innovations that can save lives and increase the value of our health care dollars. We need to revamp our system for paying health care providers—reform that will reward high-quality

# Problems with Current Health Care

An estimated 116 million adults were uninsured or underinsured, reported a medical bill problem, and/or did not access needed health care because of cost, 2007.

**177 million adults, ages 19–64**

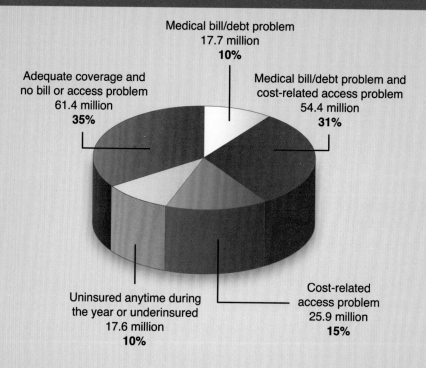

Medical bill/debt problem
17.7 million
**10%**

Adequate coverage and no bill or access problem
61.4 million
**35%**

Medical bill/debt problem and cost-related access problem
54.4 million
**31%**

Uninsured anytime during the year or underinsured
17.6 million
**10%**

Cost-related access problem
25.9 million
**15%**

Taken from: S.R. Collins, J.L. Kriss, M.M. Doty, and S.D. Rustgi, *Losing Ground: How the Loss of Adequate Health Insurance Is Burdening Working Families: Findings from the Commonwealth Fund Biennial Health Insurance Surveys*, 2001–2007, The Commonwealth Fund, August 2008.

care and prudent stewardship of resources, move toward shared provider accountability for the total care of patients, and correct the imbalance in payment whereby specialty care is rewarded more than primary or preventive care.

*Organize our care delivery systems.* We need to reorganize the delivery of care, moving from our current fragmented system to one where physicians and other care providers are rewarded for banding together into integrated or virtual organizations capable of delivering 21st-century health care. Patients need to have easy access to appropriate care and treatment information, and providers need to be responsive to the needs of all their patients. Providers must also collaborate in delivering high-quality, high-value care, and they should receive the support needed for continuous improvement.

*Invest in a modern health system.* The U.S. lags behind other countries in the adoption of health information technology and a system of health information exchange. In such a system, patient information would be available to all providers at the point of care, as well as to patients themselves through electronic health record systems, helping to ensure that care is well coordinated. Early investment in the infrastructure of a high performance health system—including information technology, research on comparative effectiveness of drugs, devices, and procedures, data on provider performance on quality and affordability, and a workforce that ensures a team approach to care—is an essential building block.

*Ensure strong national leadership.* None of the above will be possible if government does not take the lead. The federal government—the nation's largest purchaser of health care services—has tremendous leverage to effect changes in coverage, care delivery, and payment. National leadership can encourage the collaboration and coordination among private-sector leaders and government officials that are necessary to set and achieve national goals for a high performance health system. It can also help set priorities and targets for improvement, create a system for monitoring and reporting on performance, and issue recommendations on the practices and policies.

## EVALUATING THE AUTHORS' ARGUMENTS:

In this viewpoint Davis argues that the American health care system is in crisis. What problem does she identify that could be compatible with Michael D. Tanner's positive experience of the U.S. health care system?

# The Problems with America's Health Care System Are Exaggerated

> *"Our health care system is not perfect, but it has been a major source of advances in our standard of living."*

N. Gregory Mankiw

In the following viewpoint N. Gregory Mankiw argues that the problems with the U.S. health care system are often exaggerated. Mankiw denies that the statistics on life expectancy and infant mortality are related to health care. Additionally, he claims that the number of uninsured Americans does not accurately reflect the number of Americans who cannot afford insurance. Finally, Mankiw says that the high costs of health care illustrate the advances in health care rather than a problem with the health care system. Mankiw is professor of economics at Harvard University and a visiting scholar at the American Enterprise Institute for Public Policy Research (AEI). He is the author of two economics textbooks, *Principles of Economics* and *Macroeconomics*.

**AS YOU READ, CONSIDER THE FOLLOWING QUESTIONS:**
1. According to the author, what are the different infant mortality rates for America and Canada?
2. The estimated 47 million uninsured in the United States includes the numbers for how many uninsured illegal aliens, according to the author?
3. What percent of U.S. national income is spent on health care today, according to Mankiw?

With the health care system at the center of the political debate, a lot of scary claims are being thrown around. The dangerous ones are not those that are false; watchdogs in the news media are quick to debunk them. Rather, the dangerous ones are those that are true but do not mean what people think they mean.

Here are three of the true but misleading statements about health care that politicians and pundits love to use to frighten the public:

*Statement 1: The United States has lower life expectancy and higher infant mortality than Canada, which has national health insurance.*

The differences between the neighbors are indeed significant. Life expectancy at birth is 2.6 years greater for Canadian men than for American men, and 2.3 years greater for Canadian women than American women. Infant mortality in the United States is 6.8 per 1,000 live births, versus 5.3 in Canada.

These facts are often taken as evidence for the inadequacy of the American health system. But a recent study by June and Dave O'Neill, economists at Baruch College, from which these numbers come, shows that the difference in health outcomes has more to do with broader social forces.

## Life Expectancy

For example, Americans are more likely than Canadians to die by accident or by homicide. For men in their twenties, mortality rates are more than 50 percent higher in the United States than in Canada, but the O'Neills show that accidents and homicides account for most of that gap. Maybe these differences have lessons for traffic laws and gun control, but they teach us nothing about our system of health care.

Americans are also more likely to be obese, leading to heart disease and other medical problems. Among Americans, 31 percent of men and 33 percent of women have a body mass index of at least 30, a definition of obesity, versus 17 percent of men and 19 percent of women in Canada. Japan, which has the longest life expectancy among major nations, has obesity rates of about 3 percent.

The causes of American obesity are not fully understood, but they involve lifestyle choices we make every day, as well as our system of food delivery. Research by Harvard economists David Cutler, Ed Glaeser, and Jesse Shapiro concludes that America's growing obesity problem is largely attributable to our economy's ability to supply high-calorie foods cheaply. Lower prices increase food consumption, sometimes beyond the point of optimal health.

## Infant Mortality

Infant mortality rates also reflect broader social trends, including the prevalence of infants with low birth weight. The health system in the United States gives low birth-weight babies slightly better survival chances than does Canada's, but the more pronounced difference is the frequency of these cases. In the United States, 7.5 percent of babies are born weighing less than 2,500 grams (about 5.5 pounds), compared with 5.7 percent in Canada. In both nations, these infants have more than ten times the mortality rate of larger babies. Low birth weights are in turn correlated with teenage motherhood. (One theory is that a teenage mother is still growing and thus competing with the fetus for nutrients.) The rate of teenage motherhood, according to the O'Neill study, is almost three times higher in the United States than it is in Canada.

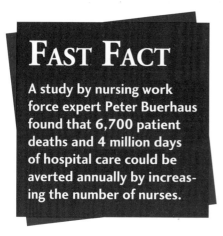

**FAST FACT**

A study by nursing work force expert Peter Buerhaus found that 6,700 patient deaths and 4 million days of hospital care could be averted annually by increasing the number of nurses.

Whatever its merits, a Canadian-style system of national health insurance is unlikely to change the sexual mores of American youth.

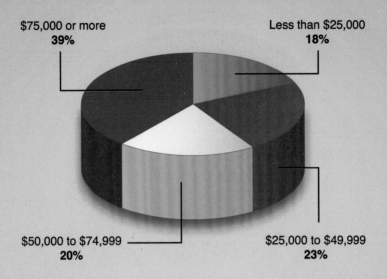

$75,000 or more
39%

Less than $25,000
18%

$50,000 to $74,999
20%

$25,000 to $49,999
23%

Taken from: U.S. Census Bureau, "Income, Poverty, and Health Insurance Coverage in the United States: 2007," www.census.gov, August 2008.

The bottom line is that many statistics on health outcomes say little about our system of health care.

## The Uninsured

*Statement 2: Some 47 million Americans do not have health insurance.*

This number from the Census Bureau is often cited as evidence that the health system is failing for many American families. Yet by masking tremendous heterogeneity in personal circumstances, the figure exaggerates the magnitude of the problem.

To start with, the 47 million includes about 10 million residents who are not American citizens. Many are illegal immigrants. Even if we had national health insurance, they would probably not be covered.

The number also fails to take full account of Medicaid, the government's health program for the poor. For instance, it counts millions of the poor who are eligible for Medicaid but have not yet applied. These individuals, who are healthier, on average, than those who are

*The author argues that because Americans are more likely to be obese and more susceptible to heart disease and other medical problems than people in other industrialized nations, it skews statistics on health care.*

enrolled, could always apply if they ever needed significant medical care. They are uninsured in name only.

The 47 million also includes many who could buy insurance but have not. The Census Bureau reports that 18 million of the uninsured have annual household incomes of more than $50,000, which puts them in the top half of the income distribution. About a quarter of the uninsured have been offered employer-provided insurance but declined coverage.

Of course, millions of Americans have trouble getting health insurance. But they number far less than 47 million, and they make up only a few percent of the population of 300 million.

Any reform should carefully focus on this group to avoid disrupting the vast majority for whom the system is working. We do not nationalize an industry simply because a small percentage of the workforce is unemployed. Similarly, we should be wary of sweeping reforms of our health system if they are motivated by the fact that a small percentage of the population is uninsured.

## Health Care Costs

*Statement 3: Health costs are eating up an ever increasing share of American incomes.*

In 1950, about 5 percent of U.S. national income was spent on health care, including both private and public health spending. Today the share is about 16 percent. Many pundits regard the increasing cost as evidence that the system is too expensive.

But increasing expenditures could just as well be a symptom of success. The reason that we spend more than our grandparents did is not waste, fraud, and abuse, but advances in medical technology and growth in incomes. Science has consistently found new ways to extend and improve our lives. Wonderful as they are, they do not come cheap.

Fortunately, our incomes are growing, and it makes sense to spend this growing prosperity on better health. The rationality of this phenomenon is stressed in a recent article by economists Charles I. Jones of the University of California, Berkeley, and Robert E. Hall of Stanford University. They ask, "As we grow older and richer, which is more valuable: a third car, yet another television, more clothing—or an extra year of life?"

Hall and Jones forecast that the share of income devoted to health care will top 30 percent by 2050. But in their model, this is not a problem—it is the modern form of progress.

Even if the rise in health care spending turns out to be less than they forecast, it is important to get reform right. Our health care system is not perfect, but it has been a major source of advances in our standard of living, and it will be a large share of the economy we bequeath to our children. As we look at reform plans, we should be careful not to be fooled by statistics into thinking that the problems we face are worse than they really are.

**EVALUATING THE AUTHORS' ARGUMENTS:**

In this viewpoint Mankiw argues that the problems with the U.S. health care system are exaggerated. Do Mankiw's claims support or undermine the arguments of Michael D. Tanner and Karen Davis, the authors of the previous viewpoints in this chapter? In what way?

Viewpoint
4

# Health Care Should Be a Right

## Daniel Zhou

> *"Healthcare is a necessity for every human being."*

In the following viewpoint Daniel Zhou argues that health care is a basic right that needs to be protected by the government in the United States. Zhou claims that problems in the United States with rising health insurance costs result in many people being uninsured. Zhou recounts a personal story of his father's experience with the health care system, which ultimately ended in his father seeking health care in China. Zhou is worried that the United States has a health care system that is inferior to that of developing countries, including China. Zhou is a high school student in Ohio.

**AS YOU READ, CONSIDER THE FOLLOWING QUESTIONS:**
1. What do companies do about health care programs in the face of rising premiums, according to the author?
2. How much does the author report that his father's brain tumor surgery cost in the United States?
3. How much did his father's brain tumor surgery cost in China, according to Zhou?

Daniel Zhou, "Life or Death," *The Nation*, December 16, 2008. Reproduced by permission.

The Constitution protects the basic inalienable rights given to the people of the United States. What is lacking from the basic rights is healthcare. Healthcare is a necessity for every human being. It is the only thing that will decide whether a person will live or die. The United States is supposed to help every person in need, but insurance companies limit the care that a person can receive from facilities like hospitals.

*In this viewpoint the author relates his and his father's experiences with the U.S. health care system and the Chinese system. He believes the U.S. health care system is in many ways inferior to the Chinese.*

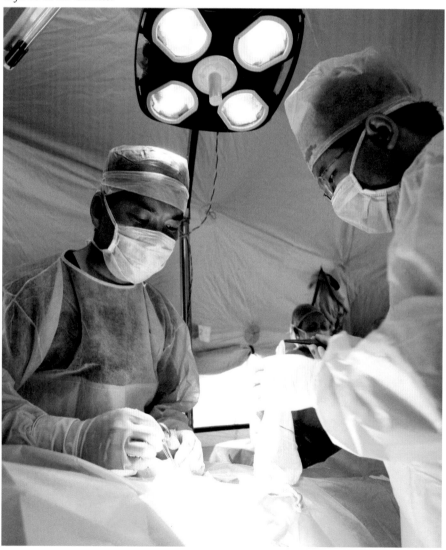

## The Health Insurance Problem

As the United States is moving from a manufacturing economy toward a service economy, healthcare insurance is becoming less stable. Due to rising premiums, companies often are unable to afford healthcare programs. Therefore, they either drop coverage completely or force their employees to pay an excessive extra share for their healthcare plan. As a result, many people are unable to keep their plans.

There are nearly 50 million people uninsured in the United States, and experts calculate that 18,000 Americans will die simply because they are uninsured. Though the United States spends more on healthcare than any other wealthy, industrialized country in the world, it is the only one that does not ensure that all its citizens have insurance. The new president [Barack Obama] must take immediate action toward fixing the corrupt healthcare system.

## A Personal Experience

My father was diagnosed with a brain tumor. In September 2007, he had his first surgery at a nationally renowned hospital. The doctor who treated my father is also nationally renowned. With the tumor at a very dangerous position, the surgery was considered to be major. Without any prehospitalized care, my dad was forced to arrive at the hospital very early in the morning the day of the surgery. The surgery took an unusually long ten hours, with only one surgeon. After being put in the intensive care unit, my father was released from the hospital two days later. There was a minimum amount of care for my father after his surgery, and the hospital practically forced him to leave two days later. A few days

> **FAST FACT**
>
> The Kaiser Family Foundation Health Care in America 2006 Survey found that 80 percent of the public is dissatisfied with the total cost of care in the nation, including 58 percent who are very dissatisfied with costs.

after arriving home, with my father still in need of care and rest, we received multiple phone calls from the hospital billing center, which demanded money right away. The total cost of the surgery, including help from the insurance company, was about $200,000. Unfortunately,

# Poll on Health Insurance Priorities

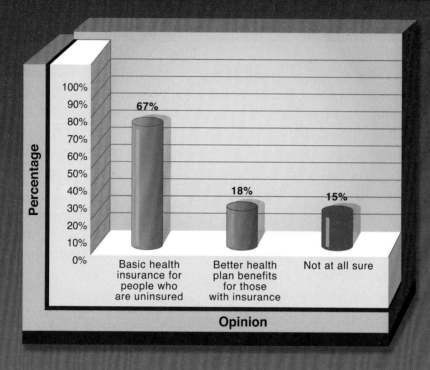

"Which should be the more important priority regarding health insurance?"

Taken from: Harris Interactive, "Health Insurance Companies Get the Most Blame for Increasing Cost of Health Care," October 16–20, 2008.

the surgery was unsuccessful. The only words that the doctor gave my dad before leaving the hospital were "Rest, or call 911."

With no help at all from the healthcare system, my father was forced to look for a second chance for surgery elsewhere. With extreme limitations on his coverage, he decided to try his home country. After arriving in China, the doctors spent a whole week just running tests and having discussions. Before the surgery, the hospital asked for an $8,000 deposit. Unlike in the states, a team of surgeons worked together during his second surgery. After a difficult nine hours, the tumor was 100 percent removed, and my dad was asked to stay for at least ten days under hospital supervision. After leaving the hospital, the nurses called him every day for a week, just to make sure he was taking the correct amount of medicine and that there were no complications, and to remind him when to return to the hospital for checkups and tests. The total cost of this surgery was $6,500, of which the hospital returned $1,500 of the original deposit.

## An Anomaly Among Developed Countries

Today in the United States, healthcare has become so unreliable and expensive that lots of people cannot afford it, which is what the next president needs to fix immediately. Healthcare coverage is usually guaranteed through employers, but as changes in insurance company policies occur, people have become less dependent on them. Free healthcare has been utilized in all the developed countries besides the United States. Although the United States should not be compared with developing countries such as China, China still has proven to have a better and more affordable healthcare system than that of the United States. My story depicts only one case, but it represents the voices of those who agree with me. We see our great country deteriorating day by day, and we hope our next president will step in and take some actions to justify our healthcare system. This is the basic, moral human need.

**EVALUATING THE AUTHOR'S ARGUMENTS:**

In this viewpoint Zhou argues that health care is a right and that the government ought to ensure that all citizens have access to health care. Can you think of at least one other right that U.S. citizens have that the government protects?

# Health Care Should Not Be Treated as a Right

Lee Hieb

"*No, health care is not a right. It is a service, just like the food service, or transportation. They may be important to our lives—hey, food is more critical than medicine. But they are not rights.*"

In the following viewpoint, Lee Hieb argues that health care should not be considered a right. Hieb contends that the founding fathers of America "recognized only 'inalienable rights'" and empowered the government to protect those rights through armed forces and police. But, Hieb suggests, enforcing the "right" of health care will force doctors to work under slavelike conditions and deprive citizens of their property through taxation, thereby violating their inalienable rights. According to Hieb, health care is a service, not a right. Furhermore, Hieb contends, the U.S. system of health care is better and faster than the systems in Sweden, Britain, and Canada that politicians are using as models for reform. Hieb concludes with the observation that "politicians who devise these government run systems never have to live with the consequences." Barack Obama, as an example, can avoid such consequences as "mediocre medicine" and "insure his own right to seek out what privilege brings." Lee Hieb is an orthopedic surgeon in solo private practice.

**AS YOU READ, CONSIDER THE FOLLOWING QUESTIONS:**
1. What are the "inalienable rights" that Hieb refers to?
2. What is the percentage of people in Britain versus the percentage of people in North Carolina who had brain imaging within 24 hours to confirm a diagnosis of a stroke?
3. According to Hieb, under what conditions does universal health care work well, and under what conditions does it fail?

At last night's presidential debate, Barack Obama led the charge for government run health care by declaring in no uncertain terms that health care is a "right". I suppose he thinks Tom and the boys accidentally left that one out of the Constitution. Or maybe it is an extension (in his mind) of the right to life.

But let's think about this a minute. When our American form of government was created to form "a more perfect union" by insuring the "rights" of its citizens, it recognized only the "inalienable rights". And to protect those rights, which I'm pretty sure only included life, liberty and the pursuit of happiness, the government was empowered to use force if necessary.

We created armed forces (and finally an adequate border patrol) to protect our people's life and liberty from foreign invasion, and then police to protect our pursuit of happiness in the form of private property. So how will we insure medical care?

We can pay for care—we've begun doing that in Medicare and Medicaid. We can set up an army of doctors to attend the unattended. We have done that in the form of Public Health Service scholarships that recruit medical students, who, after graduation work in inner cities, reservations, and prisons, etc. But ultimately, when inducements fail, will we draft young people to become doctors and nurses to fill the need to supply medical services? Will we shackle doctors at the job for 36 hours at a time, without sleep or food because there are not enough physicians to meet the "rights" of the people? Will we violate truly inalienable rights of our citizens by taking more and more of their private property through taxation to pay for an inefficient system of government run health care?

No, health care is not a right. It is a service, just like the food service, or transportation. They may be important to our lives—hey, food is more critical than medicine. But they are not rights. We cannot demand food at the grocery store, and pay according to our ability. We cannot force a car dealer to sell us a car at "Medicare" discount rates because we need transportation to get us to work.

Barack Obama is a smart guy. He's Ivy League–educated and is surrounded by a bevy of similarly bright educated people. Yet he promotes a policy that has failed everywhere it has been tried—Universal Health Care.

Now I grant you that there are other bright people who believe in this Universal Health Care nonsense, but most are taken in by the slogans and cosmic ideals—they have not really delved into the historical details. Viewed from 30,000 feet a cesspool may look like a sylvan lake. Sweden looks reasonably good if you look at global numbers such as perinatal mortality—but this does not disclose the nightmare in Swedish Emergency Rooms where children die for lack of nurses to administer an IV. In Britain, only 42% of patients had brain imaging to confirm their diagnosis of stroke within 24 hours of the onset of symptoms—a number they themselves deemed "unacceptably low". By contrast, a study in North Carolina was distressed that only 11% of people had a CT scan within 25 minutes! Over 44% had a CT within 2 hours, and by 24 hours over 60–70% of patients in the US will have received a CT scan.

## FAST FACT

The average salary for a family physician in the United Kingdom, under their national health plan, is approximately $45,000, whereas the average salary for a family physician in the United States is approximately $131,000.

We continue to hear how miserable American medical care is, and how expensive it is. Yes, there are problems—some that are inevitable, and most dating to the sixties' advent of Medicare and Medicaid. It is fine to look for improvements, but why do Barack, and his predecessor Kerry, look to socialized Europe or Canada for solutions? During peak times, an American may wait 6 hours to be seen in the ER. In Montreal, he would be on a gurney in the hall for three days. The Organization for Economic Cooperation and Development (OECD) ranks Canada in the bottom third of

Doctors in Maryland rally to demand
the Maryland General Assembly fix the
state's health care system. The author says
that preserving the incentive to practice
medicine is an important consideration
that must be decided politically.

its 29 member countries for availability of medical technology such as MRI and CT scanners. In fact, there are more MRI scanners in Seattle than in all of British Columbia. And, Canadians are not getting this poor access to care at a discount. The OECD ranked Canada fifth (out of 29 member countries) in national health expenditures in 1997.

Universal health care appeals to the well, but fails the sick. Socialized systems allow young, generally healthy people to obtain free low level medical care. But God help you if you need surgery! You'll wait a year in socialized countries for total joint replacement, and the Ontario Medical Society's official recommendation, at one point, was to leave the country to get a cardiac catheterization because you might die while waiting in Ontario.

Unfortunately the right answer is not amenable to a sound bite as is the call for free and universal health care. The answer is returning to the free market medical system, which was in place before 1962. Senator McCain is correct in proposing removing tax breaks from corporate health plans. In the past, insurance was insurance, not pre-paid health care. You, not your employer, owned the insurance. You could buy the type and level of insurance you wanted and could afford. You, not your employer, was the insurance customer, so you could vote with your feet against bad policies. (We didn't need a patient's bill of rights, nor a portability act until corporations owned your health insurance.) And you didn't expect insurance to pay for every runny nose or stubbed toe. Charity hospitals, family, and private altruism—not the government—helped to care for the indigent.

The final truth is, politicians who devise these government run systems never have to live with the consequences. Barack Obama will never wait in a crowded inner city Emergency Room. When Boris Yeltsin had his open-heart surgery—he didn't go to the lousy Soviet universal care hospital, but to a hospital just for the politburo. His Russian doctors were American trained, and even then, he flew Dr. Debakey from Texas to supervise. He knew intuitively what Ayn Rand had stated was true—"It is not safe to trust your life to a man whose life you have throttled." Trust me, Barack will declare you have a "right" to mediocre medicine, but he will insure his own right to seek out what privilege brings.

## EVALUATING THE AUTHORS' ARGUMENTS:

In this viewpoint, Hieb argues that health care is not a right. But Daniel Zhou in the previous viewpoint argues that health care is a basic right. Compare and contrast their arguments. Are there any points about health care that they agree on? What is the evidence each brings forward for or against the right to health care? Which author makes the stronger argument? Can you find other authors to support each side?

# Chapter 2

# What Issues Are Impacting Health Care in America?

*Rising costs in health care affect every American family.*

# The Insurance Industry Is Problematic

*"The United States has met an enemy it dares not confront— the American private health insurance industry."*

**Barbara Ehrenreich**

In the following viewpoint Barbara Ehrenreich argues that the private health insurance companies of the current U.S. health care system are enemies that need to be fought. Ehrenreich contends that private health insurance companies do much damage because their way of making money is contingent on denying claims, which prevents people from getting medical treatment they need and, in some cases, ends in death. Ehrenreich believes that reform of the health care system must involve the abolition of private health insurance companies. Ehrenreich is a journalist, author, and activist. She is the author of *This Land Is Their Land: Reports from a Divided Nation.*

**AS YOU READ, CONSIDER THE FOLLOWING QUESTIONS:**

1. According to Ehrenreich, what is essentially wrong with most Democratic proposals to reform health care?
2. What figure does the author cite as the amount spent on private health insurance in 2007?
3. How many Americans die each year because they cannot afford or cannot qualify for health insurance, according to Ehrenreich?

Bow your heads and raise the white flags. After facing down the Third Reich, the Japanese Empire, the U.S.S.R., Manuel Noriega and Saddam Hussein, the United States has met an enemy it dares not confront—the American private health insurance industry.

With the courageous exception of Dennis Kucinich, the Democratic candidates have all rolled out health "reform" plans that represent total, Chamberlain-like, appeasement. Edwards and Obama propose universal health insurance plans that would in no way ease the death grip of Aetna, Unicare, MetLife, and the rest of the evil-doers. Clinton—why are we not surprised?—has gone even further, borrowing the Republican idea of actually feeding the private insurers by making it mandatory to buy their product. Will I be arrested if I resist paying $10,000 a year for a private policy laden with killer co-pays and deductibles?

It's not only the Democratic candidates who are capitulating. The surrender-buzz is everywhere. I heard it from a notable liberal political scientist on a panel in August: We can't just leap to a single payer system, he said in so many words, because it would be too disruptive, given the size of the private health insurance industry. Then I heard it yesterday from a Chicago woman who leads a nonprofit agency serving the poor: How can we go to a Canadian-style system when the private industry has gotten so "big"?

Yes, it is big. Leighton Ku, at the Center for Budget and Policy Priorities, gave me the figure of $776 billion in expenditures on private health insurance for this year. It's also a big-time employer, paying what economist Paul Krugman has estimated two to three million people just to turn down claims.

This in turn generates ever more employment in doctors' offices to battle the insurance companies. Dr. Atul Gawande, a practicing physician, wrote in *The New Yorker* that "a well-run office can get

**FAST FACT**

According to the U.S. Census Bureau, the number of Americans without insurance has risen to 46 million, or 15 percent of the population in 2007, up from 38 million, or 14 percent, in 1999.

*The author contends that health insurance companies' practices force doctors to hire people just to battle the insurance providers over coverage and costs.*

the insurer's rejection rate down from 30 percent to, say, 15 percent. That's how a doctor makes money. It's a war with insurance, every step of the way." And that's another thing your insurance premium has to pay for: the ongoing "war" between doctors and insurers.

Note: The private health insurance industry is not big because it relentlessly seeks out new customers. Unlike any other industry, this one grows by rejecting customers. No matter how shabby you look, Cartier, Lexus, or Nordstrom's will happily take your money. Not Aetna. If you have a prior conviction—excuse me, a pre-existing condition—it doesn't want your business. Private health insurance

"OUR INSURANCE COMPANY WILL PAY!"

is only for people who aren't likely to ever get sick. In fact, why call it "insurance," which normally embodies the notion of risk-sharing? This is extortion.

Think of the damage. An estimated 18,000 Americans die every year because they can't afford or can't qualify for health insurance. That's the 9/11 carnage multiplied by three—every year. Not to mention all the people who are stuck in jobs they hate because they don't dare lose their current insurance.

Saddam Hussein never killed 18,000 Americans or anything close; nor did the U.S.S.R. Yet we faced down those "enemies" with huge patriotic bluster, vast military expenditures, and, in the case of Saddam, armed intervention. So why does the U.S. soil its pants and cower in fear when confronted with the insurance industry?

Here's a plan: First, locate the major companies. No major intelligence effort will be required, since Google should suffice. Second, estimate their armed strength. No doubt there are legions of security guards involved in protecting the company headquarters from irate consumers, but these should be manageable with a few brigades. Next, consider an air strike, followed by an infantry assault.

And what about the two to three million insurance industry employees whose sole job it is to turn down claims? Well, I have a plan for them: It's called unemployment. What country in its right mind would pay millions of people to deny other people health care?

I'm not mean, though. If we had the kind of universal, single-payer, health insurance Kucinich is advocating, private health insurance workers would continue to be covered even after they are laid off. As for the health insurance company executives, there should be an adequate job training program for them—perhaps as home health aides.

Fellow citizens, where is the old macho spirit that has sustained us through countless conflicts against enemies both real and imagined? In the case of health care, we have identified the enemy, and the time has come to crush it.

**EVALUATING THE AUTHOR'S ARGUMENTS:**

In this viewpoint Ehrenreich claims that Americans die because they are denied care by the private health insurance industry. Do you think nationalizing health care would eliminate these deaths? Explain your answer.

# The Insurance Industry Is Not Problematic

*"The slice of our enormous health care costs that can reasonably be laid at the insurers' doorstep is much, much smaller than most people believe."*

**Mark Gimein**

In the following viewpoint Mark Gimein argues that health insurance companies are wrongly charged with being the source of the problem of high health care costs. Gimein identifies and claims to refute three myths about health insurance companies. He denies that health insurance company profits are the source of high health care costs. He also claims that no evidence supports the view that the government could provide health care for less money. Finally, Gimein claims that the large size of health insurance companies actually leads to lower, not higher, health care costs. Gimein is a reporter and writer.

**AS YOU READ, CONSIDER THE FOLLOWING QUESTIONS:**
1. According to Gimein, the biggest five health insurers had profits in 2007 that amounted to what percentage of total health care costs?
2. According to the author, the Medicare Advantage program (without the added fee-for-service plans), which uses private insurers, costs what percent less than the standard government-run Medicare, all things considered?
3. What is the real reason for resistance to health insurance company mergers, according to Gimein?

Mark Gimein, "Stop Blaming the Insurers," Slate.com, April 30, 2008. Reprinted with permission of the author.

Here's what's not in dispute: The United States spends 16 percent of its national income on health care, more than any other country in the world. In return, we get lower life expectancy than most other Western countries, uneven care, and enormous anxiety about how to pay for it.

Who's to blame? Not the hospitals and doctors, or the health care consumers (that is, us) who insist on expensive and questionable elective procedures. It's big health insurers—isn't it? Easy enough: Our interactions with them are impersonal, their political clout is substantial, and their names and logos look and sound like they came out of focus-group hell.

Alas, the slice of our enormous health care costs that can reasonably be laid at the insurers' doorstep is much, much smaller than most people believe. The debate about health care tends to be informed by three notions about health insurance:

- The profits of private insurers are so big that cutting them out would meaningfully lower costs.
- Private insurance clearly costs more than a government-run system such as Medicare.
- Mergers that have created a small number of huge and powerful insurers increase health care costs.

None of these is true.

## Insurance Company Profits

*Myth No. 1: Insurers' profits are responsible for our health care costs.*

This is the most pervasive and most crowd-pleasing of the health care myths. The profits of the big health insurance companies are central to the rhetoric of the health care debate, figuring heavily in the [2008] Democratic primary campaign. [2008 Presidential candidate] Barack Obama's platform includes a promise to force insurers to spend enough on care "instead of keeping exorbitant amounts for profits and administration." Michael Moore, the director of [the documentary film] *Sicko*, has hammered the point repeatedly, thundering about how insurers maximize profits by "providing as little care as possible."

The problem here is that between them the five biggest health insurers—UnitedHealthCare, Wellpoint, Aetna, Humana, and

Cigna—which cover 105 million members, last year [2007] had profits between them of $11.8 billion. This is not a small number; these are very profitable companies. But total U.S. health care costs last year were in the area of $2.3 trillion.

So, with a membership that included a little more than half of the Americans covered by private insurance, these five insurers' profits came to 0.5 percent of total health care costs. (One interesting point of comparison: In 2006, the income earned by the 50 biggest *nonprofit* hospitals alone came out at $4 billion.)

Critics also argue that insurance companies pass along excessive administrative costs to their customers. Wellpoint, for instance, spends 18 percent of the premiums it takes in on sales and administrative costs. That represents a real concern but merely raises the next question: Can a government-run program that cuts out insurers do it for less?

## The Medicare Advantage Plan

*Myth No. 2: Evidence from Medicare shows that a government program can provide the same services for less than the insurers.*

A common argument raised in support of a national "single payer" health insurance system is the experience of Medicare Advantage, a program that gives seniors the option of replacing traditional Medicare with private insurers' HMO or "preferred provider" network plans. Nine million of the 44 million people Medicare covers have signed up. A well-publicized report by the Commonwealth Fund calculated the cost of these plans at 12 percent more than traditional Medicare. This number was picked up by the *New York Times'* Paul Krugman as an illustration of the excessive costs of private insurance. More recently, the Center on Budget and Policy Priorities, a liberal think tank, has estimated the greater cost of Medicare Advantage as more than $1,000 a year extra per beneficiary.

These accurate numbers miss the fact that Medicare Advantage's design virtually guarantees that it will be more expensive than traditional Medicare. The reason for this, however, is not the excessive cost of having private insurers administer the plans. It's the cost of inducements that government has offered seniors to join them.

The original idea behind Medicare Advantage was to reduce costs by pushing seniors into HMOs that would be able to rein in health care costs. The big incentive for seniors to join the plans is supplemental coverage similar to what's offered by Medigap plans.

The government pays insurers more than the costs of Medicare, but most of that money is (and must be, by mandate) returned to members in the form of lower deductibles and co-payments. Yes, Medicare Advantage HMO programs do cost the government more than standard Medicare.

## Standard Medicare

But guess what? Take out the cuts in costs that patients pay themselves, and, in fact, the plans cost 3 percent *less*. So in a typical state like Minnesota, where standard Medicare runs the government $666 a month for each beneficiary, the government may indeed pay about $725, but the insurer will get only $650 of that, while the member gets cuts in out-of-pocket costs of $75 a month, or about $900 a year.

This isn't the end of the story. It turns out that seniors, like just about everyone else, prefer the ordinary Medicare model—which lets them see any participating doctor—to an HMO. So Medicare Advantage added "fee for service" plans, private plans that offer flexibility—and still include the incentives. (Does this undercut the original point of the program? You bet.)

These plans do cost 9 percent more, even after taking into account the lower deductibles [the portion of an insurance claim not covered by the insurance provider] and co-payments [payments made by the patient to offset the cost of care]. But be careful about jumping on this number. Here's why: When you eliminate co-payments and lower deductibles, people go to the doctor a lot more often. According to the Government Accountability Office, seniors with Medigap coverage may cost the government as much as 25 percent more than those without. When you take that into account, it actually might be surprising that Medicare Advantage isn't still *more* expensive.

None of this means that the Medicare Advantage program is cost-efficient. The bottom line, though, is that its costs come not from insurance company inefficiency or profiteering, but from the extra benefits shoehorned into it.

## The Size of Insurance Companies
*Myth No. 3: The concentration of power in a few large insurers raises health care costs.*

*Arkansas officials unveil new advertising aimed at seniors, explaining the benefits and inducements of the Medicare Advantage Plan.*

Politicians and doctors' groups blame the mergers of many smaller insurance companies into a few behemoths for rapidly increasing premiums. Big insurance mergers have been vigorously opposed by the politicians in California who fought against the huge Anthem-Wellpoint merger, and in New York. In Nevada, Gov. Jim Gibbons has said a merger of two big insurers would "take money out of the pockets of consumers and physicians." The American Medical Association has put what it calls "anti-trust reform" among the top items on its agenda.

We should be wary of mergers driving up the premiums that insurers can charge. But that fear is not the real reason why the American Medical Association has vociferously lobbied to put the brakes on mergers. That reason is the other, bigger effect of consolidation: It lowers the reimbursement rates that insurers give to doctors and hospitals. The hospital you go to and the doctor you see face to face might be more sympathetic than the health insurers, but they are a much larger part of the health care cost equation.

How big is this effect? One measure: Reimbursement rates from major insurers in Pennsylvania for some procedures have fallen to just 85 percent of the already low Medicare rates. And what makes it even worse for doctors (and, yes, potentially better for health care costs) is that insurers' contracts often have a "most favored rates" clause. If one huge insurance company can squeeze hospitals for better prices, then others are entitled to the same deal.

Whether, in fact, doctors and hospitals are unfairly pressed by giant insurance companies is a debate that may be worth having. And maybe the insurance companies' power should be reduced. But that would lead to higher, not lower, costs.

## Diagnosis

Patient, heal thyself. It's not insurers that push expensive drugs, long-shot end-of-life treatments, and redundant procedures. It's customers who ask for them. And mainly doctors and hospitals who profit. How to deal with those issues is a question that will affect the health care bottom line more than whether it's the government or private companies that provide insurance. Too bad it's one we have hardly even started to answer.

# Employers Need to Be More Involved in Health Care

**Michael E. Porter, Elizabeth O. Teisberg, and Scott Wallace**

*"Employers have a strategic role to play in improving value in the health care system."*

In the following viewpoint Michael E. Porter, Elizabeth O. Teisberg, and Scott Wallace argue that employers need to be more involved in the health care of their employees. Rather than thinking in terms of cost of the health benefits of employees, the authors encourage employers to think more in terms of value, and they identify several things employers can do to this end. Porter is the Bishop William Lawrence University Professor at Harvard Business School and coauthor of *Redefining Health Care: Creating Value-Based Competition on Results.* Teisberg is an associate professor of business at University of Virginia's Darden School of Business, a senior fellow at the New England Healthcare Institute, and coauthor of *Redefining Health Care: Creating Value-Based Competition on Results.* Wallace is a fellow at the Batten Institute at University of Virginia's Darden School of Business.

Michael E. Porter, Elizabeth O. Teisberg, and Scott Wallace, "Rethinking the Role of Employers," *Financial Times,* July 3, 2008. Reproduced by permission of the authors.

What should employers do about healthcare? In the US, they have often treated health benefits as a necessary evil. They have focused on the rising cost of providing health insurance benefits and taken aggressive steps to bring costs down, or at least to slow the rate of increase.

In many other countries, employers have ignored healthcare altogether, leaving it to government or dutifully paying their mandated health contributions. Many US employers are dropping health benefits or hoping for reforms that will transfer responsibility for health insurance to individuals or to the government.

## How Health Care Affects Employers

Think again. Employers cannot get out of healthcare, no matter what kind of health insurance system is put in place. They bear the cost of poor health in the form of sick days, absenteeism, reduced productivity at work, and early retirements of skilled contributors. Recent internal company studies in the US estimate that employers spend 200 to 300 per cent more on the indirect costs of poor health than they do on health benefits. The costs of poor health are especially high for chronic conditions such as diabetes, migraines, heart disease and respiratory problems. These costs remain even if employers get out of health insurance obligations. But by disengaging, employers lose much of their ability to influence the costs of poor health.

This is what many European companies have discovered. In Sweden, for example, excessive rates of absenteeism in the 1980s caused many companies seriously to focus on increasing employee attendance and productivity through comprehensive health and wellness programs.

What is the best way for employers to address their health benefits issues? Here again, fuzzy thinking has made the problem worse. In every other aspect of their business, employers are attuned to quality and value. But healthcare has been treated as a commodity and cost reduction has been the dominant approach.

Employers have gone to their vendors, health plans or third-party administrators in the case of self insured plans, and tried to bargain the maximum discounts. They have switched plans frequently in search of a better deal, which has meant that their employees need-

## Average Employee and Employer Contributions to Health Care Premiums, 2000–2007

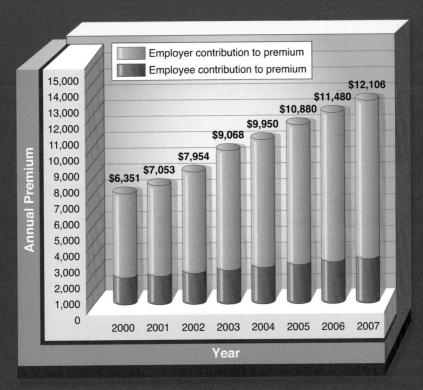

Average annual firm and worker contribution and total premiums (shown above bar) for family coverage.

Taken from: Kaiser Family Foundation HRET Employer Health Benefits Surveys, 2000–2007; AFL-CIO, "Health Insurance Costs Cripple Employers," www.aflcio.org/issues/healthcare/facts_employers.cfm.

ed to switch as well. They have tried to pare back covered services, thrown up barriers to expensive drugs and treatments, and recently, begun to pass more and more costs on to employees.

Yet health benefit costs have continued to go up. Most employers do not even measure the costs of poor health among their employees. If they did, however, they would discover that many of the steps they have taken to reduce benefit costs have actually made the costs of poor health even greater. For example, studies have shown that co-pays and deductibles on essential medications for chronic conditions can reduce adherence to therapy, leading to expensive hospitalisations, complications and the like. Here, so-called consumer-driven health plans not only failed to benefit the consumer, but they hurt employers as well.

## Prioritizing Value over Cost

What to do? The most important single change necessary is for employers to think about healthcare in terms of value, not cost. Value is the health outcomes achieved for the money spent. Cost includes not only the immediate, short-term costs of treatment but the long-term costs of ongoing care as well as the indirect cost of poor health. The goal should be to increase value, not reduce the short-term costs of health benefits. New research on value-based health care delivery reveals some powerful, and ultimately optimistic, principles.

First, the best way truly to reduce healthcare cost is to improve its quality—better diagnoses, more timely treatment, less invasive methods, getting the right treatment to the right patient, fewer complications, and so on. Quality, defined in terms of outcomes, is the secret to success in healthcare.

Second, high-value care is delivered by integrated practice units including all the needed specialities that care for the patient's medical condition over the full cycle of care, not the current model organised and paid for by specialty and discrete interventions.

Third, prevention and screening can dramatically improve value, as does ongoing disease management to prevent recurrences and setbacks.

Fourth, the only way truly to drive value is to measure patient outcomes for each medical condition, and get patients to providers who have the scale, experience, teams and facilities to achieve excellent results.

## What Employers Can Do

To move to a value-based approach to employee health benefits, employers must take a number of essential steps. The first is to mount an aggressive approach to wellness, prevention, screening, and active management of chronic conditions. Here, many employers in the US and Europe have made impressive starts. Some companies cover the costs of smoking cessation and weight loss programmes, or reward participation in health and risk assessment screenings. To encourage healthy lifestyle choices, employers offer fitness programmes and healthy menu choices in company cafeterias, sometimes at lower prices than the less healthy alternatives. To promote screening and management of chronic conditions, employers are moving to on-site clinics to enable convenient vaccinations, convenient ongoing monitoring, and care for routine health issues. On-site physical therapists offer coaching to prevent injury and services to speed recovery. On-site diabetes educators work with groups of employees to engage them in lifestyle changes that prevent disease progression. Co-payments are eliminated for medications and services used to treat chronic conditions.

Companies are tracking the ROIs [return on investment] of these investments in health with good results. These kind of health and wellness initiatives are a great place to start. And, they are not enough.

Second, employers need to directly engage in improving the structure of healthcare delivery, and thus its quality. This begins with redefining relationships with health plans away from cost reduction and discounts to quality and value. Employers must expect health plans to direct patients to excellent providers, not those provider networks that offer the biggest discounts. Employers need health plans to encourage integrated practice units, and assemble comprehensive health information for members. Today's practice of paying health plan administrators a percentage of the company's healthcare costs undermines value, as does restricting provider networks based on the

> **FAST FACT**
>
> According to the Commonwealth Fund, sickness and health problems among working-age Americans and their families carry an estimated price tag of $260 billion in lost productivity each year.

*Employer-based wellness programs that focus on fitness and prevention help cut costs and are popular with employees.*

size of discounts. Some employers are already contracting directly with integrated provider organisations for care of complex conditions such as cancer, organ failure, heart disease, or diabetes. They should expect their health plans to do so as well. In Germany, for example, a sick fund and a hospital worked together to create an integrated practice unit for migraine care. In the first six months, absenteeism for migraine sufferers was reduced from 57 per cent who missed a week of work or more per year to 11 per cent.

## Measuring Outcomes and Ensuring Change

Third, employers need to drive outcome measurement throughout the system. Business leaders know that what is measured will improve. A critical step is to expect outcome measurement by providers for each medical condition, adjusted for patient population. Over time, outcome measures should be defined and collected as a matter of national policy. Employers can no longer be satisfied with current process compliance measures and overly broad metrics covering hospitals as a whole. What is needed is true outcomes, medical condition by medical condition, that will guide choice of providers and enable clinicians to improve. Employers must also expect that health plans and health plan administrators measure and improve their health results for plan members.

Fourth, employers must accelerate change in reimbursement to link financial success to clinical success. Today, providers are paid by visit, by speciality, and by procedure, or through DRGs (diagnosis-related groups) that are too narrow to encompass the necessary care. Reimbursement must shift to bundled payments covering the total care of the patient's medical condition, including all the specialties and services involved. Only in this way is reimbursement aligned with value, and rewards providers for innovations that improve health and reduce the need for more care or more complex care. In the US, employers may need to contract directly with providers if health plans are slow to modify their flawed contracting practices. Worldwide, employers should support efforts to realign payment systems with value.

It is high time for employers to stop complaining about healthcare and modify their own practices that are perpetuating the system's problems. Employers' interests and employees' interests are closely aligned around a common goal when it comes to healthcare—better health. Employers have a strategic role to play in improving value in the health care system. Rather than disenfranchising employers, policymakers would be well advised to harness this role. Employers, for their part, need to recognise their fundamental interest in the health of their employees and act on it.

## EVALUATING THE AUTHORS' ARGUMENTS:

In this viewpoint Porter, Teisberg, and Wallace argue that employers ought to be more involved in the health care of employees. How do you think the author of the next viewpoint, Clive Crook, would respond to this?

# Employers Need to Be Less Involved in Health Care

## Clive Crook

> *"Employers do not insure your house or your car; why should they insure your health?"*

In the following viewpoint Clive Crook argues that the current U.S. health care system where employers are heavily involved in providing health care insurance to employees is wrongheaded. Crook believes that proposed health care system reforms by both Republicans and Democrats rely too heavily on employer-provided health insurance to be successful at driving down cost. Rather than endorsing a single-payer government-run health care system, Crook instead believes that using market forces, consumer autonomy, and government vouchers will move employers away from providing health care insurance and, at the same time, lower health care costs. Crook is a senior editor of the *Atlantic Monthly*, a columnist for *National Journal*, and a commentator for the *Financial Times*.

Clive Crook, "Fact and Fiction in Health Care Reform," *National Journal*, vol. 39, June 9, 2007, pp. 20–21. Copyright © 2009 by National Journal Group Inc. All rights reserved. Reprinted with permission from *National Journal*.

**AS YOU READ, CONSIDER THE FOLLOWING QUESTIONS:**
1. According to the author, what are the two main challenges to fixing the U.S. health care system?
2. What does Crook cite as the reason American doctors would not want the U.S. health care system to be modeled after the French health care system?
3. What is the reason that employers are involved in providing health insurance to employees, according to Crook?

The Democratic Party's presidential candidates all believe that health care reform will help them in 2008. So far, only John Edwards and Barack Obama have presented detailed proposals (and Obama's is not all that detailed when you look closely), but every Democrat in the race has plenty to say on the subject. In Mitt Romney, meanwhile, the Republicans have a candidate who helped enact a universal health care plan as governor of Massachusetts, and is proud to say so. Still wary of "socialized medicine," he and the rest of the GOP field see widespread concern about the rising cost of health care. Like the Democratic candidates, they all promise to do something about it if elected.

In short, the politics of health care is once again coming to the boil. Something may even happen.

The second Democratic presidential debate was revealing. Hillary Rodham Clinton has been tentative on the subject up to now, anxious not to inflame memories of the "Hillarycare" fiasco of 1994. She has not yet announced a plan, but she showed no embarrassment or hesitation last Sunday, no steering off the subject at all.

To the contrary, her command of the issue was on bold display, packaged in a tacit acknowledgment that the Clinton administration got the politics (not the substance) wrong and that she had learned lessons. Articles insisting that she was right on health care all along have been appearing for a while now, and the idea no longer gets a laugh. (The most recent and most impressively argued of these is a piece by Jonathan Cohn in *The New Republic*.) The mood has shifted. When it comes to working out the details, health care may still be a political minefield, but all of the presidential candidates are preparing to march in.

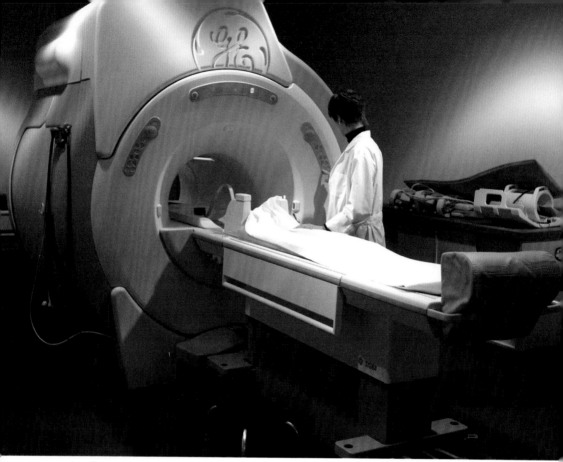

*A technician operates an MRI machine in Canada. The author points to the problems in the Canadian government's health care system as an argument against government-run health care.*

This is a good thing. The country's health care system is needlessly expensive and needlessly unfair. In terms of aggregate health outcomes, it is not particularly effective. It leaves tens of millions uninsured and makes many of those who *are* insured anxious about future loss of coverage and the financial catastrophe that might ensue. It locks people into jobs they might otherwise leave, puts an immense financial and administrative burden on companies, and saps the country's economic vitality. It is broken and needs fixing.

The two main challenges are easily stated: Curb rapidly accelerating costs and achieve universal coverage. But those goals push in opposite directions. How can you cut costs and also cover more people? A variety of sleights of hand are being proposed, with differences attuned to partisan prejudice, to give the impression that you can pretty easily do both things at once.

Republicans are fond of arguing that the key to universal coverage is to get the price of insurance down. If only coverage were more affordable, everybody would choose to buy it. Actually they wouldn't, as is clear from other insurance markets. Many of today's uninsured could afford a health plan, but choose not to buy one.

The converse Republican illusion is to believe that mandatory universal coverage (as in the Massachusetts plan) will make insurance cheaper by bringing "free riders" into the system. Well, if insurance was cheaper, more people (not everybody) would buy it; and if everybody was herded into the system, costs per consumer would fall (a bit). In other words, cost-control and broader coverage are indeed complementary, but only to a limited degree—enough to make the cost of achieving universal health care lower than a straightforward extrapolation would suggest, but certainly not lower (other things being equal) than the cost of the current system.

Democrats sometimes borrow those arguments. Obama's plan relies heavily on affordability to broaden coverage (leading his rivals in the party to criticize it for failing to make coverage truly universal). But the principal illusion on the Democratic side is that any increase in overall costs, such as it is, can be piled without ill effect on businesses rather than on taxpayers or health care consumers. As Democrats tell it, the profits of insurance and pharmaceutical companies serve no economic purpose. They are rents arising from rigged markets: All of that money can be clawed back and set against the cost of fixing the system. If taxes still need to go up after that, employers at large can pay. No problem, they also are making too much money.

> **FAST FACT**
>
> The current tax subsidy given to employers for providing employees with health insurance costs the U.S. Treasury more than $200 billion in lost revenue, since premiums for employer-provided health coverage are excluded from income taxes and from payroll taxes.

The likelihood—indeed the certainty—that piling costs onto business will lead to higher prices, less innovation, and lower wages is never confronted. Returning the compliment, by the way, supposedly pro-enterprise Republicans are not above deploying this kind of argument. Romney's Massachusetts plan pays for near-universal coverage with new business taxes and obligations.

Those who argue for socialized medicine—for a single-payer, government-run system along British or Canadian lines—are at least being more honest and more coherent. Set the government up as a monopoly buyer of health care, and it can use its power to drive costs down. But patients have limited choice in those systems, and access is rationed. In this country, those facts cannot be waved away. Americans are unlikely to take to such restrictions—not if they are happy (as most people with coverage say they are) with their present arrangements.

The French system is an interesting hybrid, closer to that of the U.S. system than you might suppose—with patient autonomy and multiple insurance intermediaries, but mostly paid for by taxpayers and with heavy government regulation. The French system is cheaper than America's but more expensive than Britain's or Canada's. It gets good results, but helps keep France's taxes very high. And American doctors would have some reservations about adopting such a system: They are paid about three times what their French counterparts earn.

A quite different reform strategy—which I think is preferable on the merits, as well as politically more feasible—is to retain the distinctively American aspects of this system, notably its reliance on competing private providers, while in key respects strengthening, not attenuating, the power of market forces. The crux of this idea is to give consumers real choices. That in turn can happen only if employers are largely taken out of the health insurance decision.

Employers do not insure your house or your car; why should they insure your health? No reason, except that a huge tax subsidy encourages them to do so. With employers selecting plans on their behalf, most workers cannot decide for themselves how to trade benefits off against cost—whether to sign up with a health maintenance organization (with the restrictions that imposes), or to pay more for a preferred provider organization, or more still for no-restrictions coverage. If consumers lack the ability to make such choices (and, having made them, bear the consequences on cost), the health care market is hardly a market at all, and the downward pressure on costs that market discipline would otherwise supply is never going to kick in. This is

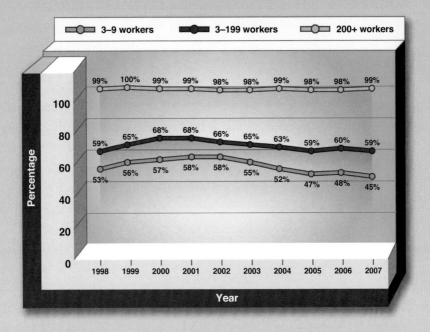

**Percentage of Employers Offering Health Benefits by Firm Size, 1996–2007**

Legend: 3–9 workers | 3–199 workers | 200+ workers

200+ workers: 99%, 100%, 99%, 99%, 98%, 98%, 99%, 98%, 98%, 99%

3–199 workers: 59%, 65%, 68%, 68%, 66%, 65%, 63%, 59%, 60%, 59%

3–9 workers: 53%, 56%, 57%, 58%, 58%, 55%, 52%, 47%, 48%, 45%

Percentage (y-axis): 0, 20, 40, 60, 80, 100

Year (x-axis): 1998, 1999, 2000, 2001, 2002, 2003, 2004, 2005, 2006, 2007

Taken from: Kaiser/HRET Survey of Employer-Sponsored Health Benefits. www.covertheuninsured.org.

to say nothing of the other great drawbacks of relying on employers (including the problem of "lock in").

The administration has proposed one useful step in this regard: extending tax relief to individually purchased plans. Much more needs to be done to push employers out of the health insurance market. Most of the reforms now being touted, by Democrats and Republicans alike, aim to do the opposite.

Using market forces and consumer autonomy to drive down costs is worth a try, in my view, but that by itself will not solve the coverage problem. I would do that by guaranteeing everybody, regardless of income or health history, a voucher that would buy a standard HMO-type plan. This could be done in a variety of ways. You could give everybody a voucher (which could be used as partial payment for a more expensive policy) and recover the cost from general taxation. Or you could give full vouchers only to people on low incomes, tapering the value to zero as incomes rose, again asking taxpayers to pick up the check—and in this case also mandating that everybody buy at least the basic plan. You could satisfy the "ignore pre-existing conditions" criterion either through regulation or by adjusting the value of vouchers according to health risk. The cost would depend on such details, and many more besides—but you can be sure it would not be small.

I can understand why no Republican contender for the presidency is proposing this. Only a very unusual Republican would suggest a significant rise in taxes to mainly benefit the least-well-off. But why is no Democrat proposing such a scheme? Because it is politically more appealing to pretend that this great and long-overdue social advance can be achieved mainly at the expense of greedy employers (and grasping insurance and pharmaceutical companies). It just ain't so. The saddest part, meanwhile, is that keeping up this pretense entrenches employer-based insurance, the very aspect of the present system that does most to inflate costs.

## EVALUATING THE AUTHORS' ARGUMENTS:

In this viewpoint Crook argues that employers should not be involved in providing health care insurance to employees. If employers were not involved in providing health insurance, which of the four suggestions for employer involvement in health care within the previous viewpoint do you think Porter, Teisberg, and Wallace would still argue should remain?

# The High Cost of Health Care Is the Result of Waste

**Wayne Laugesen**

*"The country's healthcare industry provides inefficient care because of the regulatory disconnect between provider and customer."*

In the following viewpoint the author argues in the *Appeal-Democrat* that health care is inefficient and costly, and this is because of government regulation. Several decades ago, government laws created the ability for employers to offer health insurance to employees free of tax, resulting in the current state of affairs where employers frequently provide health insurance. The problem with this third-party health coverage, the author argues, is that consumers have no incentive to pay attention to costs of health care. The author concludes that without reform the current health care system will continue to be wasteful with resources. Wayne Laugesen is an American columnist and editorial page editor for the *Colorado Springs Gazette.*

**AS YOU READ, CONSIDER THE FOLLOWING QUESTIONS:**

1. According to the author, what would good health maintenance do for the health care system?

2. In what year did the U.S. government eliminate payroll taxes on employer contributions to employee health plans?
3. What three things are needed for a maintenance-centric health care system, according to the author?

A merica's top health executives told the *Washington Post* something obvious: Healthcare isn't a bargain.

"We're not getting what we pay for," said Denis Cortese, president and chief executive of the Mayo Clinic.

"Our healthcare system is fraught with waste," said Gary Kaplan, chairman of Seattle's Virginia Mason Medical Center.

Kaiser Permanente CEO George Halvorson said American healthcare is inefficient, wasteful and dangerous.

"There is more than enough money in the system. We just are not spending it well," said former U.S. House Speaker Newt Gingrich, who runs the Center for Health Transformation.

## Interference with Market Functions

Most agree the inefficiency results from a healthcare industry that's focused more on cure than prevention. It strives to treat heart and artery disease, doing little to discourage smoking, encourage healthful diets, exercise and blood pressure maintenance. Of course this is true. Good health maintenance saves extraordinary amounts of money and reduces demand on limited healthcare resources. Just as reducing demand on oil lowers the price of oil, reducing demand for health care services would reduce the cost of health care.

**FAST FACT**

According to the Henry J. Kaiser Family Foundation, premiums for employer-based health insurance rose by 5 percent in 2008.

Potential causes of the cure-based, hospital-centric, non-maintenance health care industry include: A) A conspiracy, in which the nation's doctors, nurses and insurance executives converged in a smoke-filled room and decided to do things wrong; or B) The tax code and government regulation, which have interfered with natural market functions.

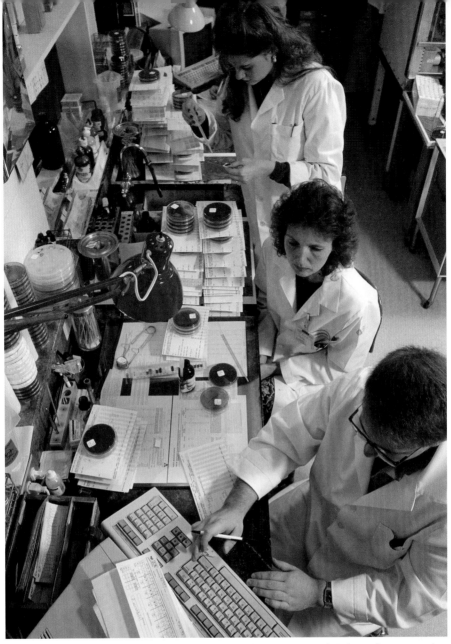

*Medical personnel spend hours a day filling out regulatory paperwork. The author cites undue regulatory paperwork and tax codes that interfere with the free market and contribute to rising costs.*

If you chose "B," congratulations! The country's healthcare industry provides inefficient care because of the regulatory disconnect between provider and customer. The system consists of few incentives for low prices and responsible consumption because most people have pre-paid health care services funded by premiums paid to insurance pools.

Americans with employer-based health plans have been lulled into a misperception that the health plan is a gift from the employer, when it's merely earned as an invisible form of compensation.

## The Source of Third-Party Health Coverage

The system dates back to 1942, when Congress and President Franklin D. Roosevelt initiated wage controls.

Businesses, needing to compete for the best employees, found that health benefits—in the form of insurance and pre-paid plans—provided a way around wage controls. That same year, the government encouraged non-cash compensation by eliminating payroll taxes on employer contributions to employee health plans. In 1943, a federal court ruled that companies could make payments to commercial insurance pools that would not be taxed as employee income. Those events established a system that lacks conventional free-market checks and balances that result from direct buyer/seller relationships.

The result of subsidized, third-party health coverage is a system in which working Americans have a surplus of pre-paid health coverage that consumes a substantial chunk of each worker's earnings. When they consume medical services, a third party pays the bill. The insured consumer doesn't even ask about the cost of an MRI, lab work, or other procedures. In fact, the more it costs the better, because it's a benefit of the job. The pre-paid and insured consumer doesn't strive to avoid the future need for expensive artery stents or bypass surgery, because a third-party payer will write the check. The arrangement eliminates any financial incentive for the consumer to avoid serious and costly health problems, and creates a bizarre incentive for consumers to consume expensive cures.

## An Analogy

Imagine if a chunk of employee compensation came in the form of pre-paid auto repair.

Millions of Americans wouldn't bother with $30 oil changes each 3,000 miles. When their engines seized, they'd tow their cars in for replacement motors or overhauls, never asking the price. A third-party would write the check, drawing on funds the customer earned but never controlled. Consumers would have incentive to consume what they had paid for, and providers would see no demand for efficient, cost-effective maintenance services. Grease Monkey and Jiffy Lube wouldn't exist.

Healthcare professionals can talk themselves silly about the need for a maintenance-centric health care system. They will never get one, however, unless it financially rewards health maintenance, financially discourages neglect, and gives patients a reason to care about the price tags on services, procedures and drugs.

## EVALUATING THE AUTHOR'S ARGUMENTS:

The author argues that the current employer-provided health care system, if applied to car care, would be to not bother with oil changes. What component of health care is like oil changes in this analogy? That is, what do health care consumers not seek out from doctors, instead waiting until they need a treatment such as bypass surgery? Do you think this is a fair analogy? Explain your answer.

# The High Cost of Health Care Is the Result of Improvement in Quality

**Don Peck**

*"Most of the growth in health-care spending has produced real improvements in the scope of medical services and the quality of care."*

In the following viewpoint Don Peck argues that U.S. health care has greatly increased in quality in the last few decades, and that this is why Americans are spending more on health care today. Peck maintains that technological innovation is the main driver of high health care costs. The fact that so many expensive innovations that increase health outcomes to any degree are now used extensively leads Peck to conclude that the only way to bring down health care costs significantly is to further ration health care, a solution that he claims is likely to be met with opposition. Peck is deputy managing editor at the *Atlantic Monthly*.

AS YOU READ, CONSIDER THE FOLLOWING QUESTIONS:
1. According to Peck, chronic disabilities for people over the age of sixty-five declined from 25 percent in 1982 to what in 1999?
2. Approximately what percentage of health care spending is for tests, treatments, and visits that have no positive effect on the quality or length of patient lives, according to the author?
3. Peck argues that the American social ethos toward health care can be described as what?

For all its flaws, medical care in the United States has improved enormously over the past several decades. Deaths from heart disease have fallen by 40 percent since 1970. In the mid-1980s HIV was an automatic death sentence; it's not anymore. Since 1990, thanks to better detection and treatment, cancer mortality rates have been falling. (Breast-cancer mortality is down by 20 percent since 1990.) Altogether, medical advances have helped to raise U.S. life expectancy from an average of sixty-eight years in 1950 to seventy-seven years today [2004].

## Improvement in American Health

Not only have American lives grown longer, but their quality has improved. The proportion of people over sixty-five with one or more chronic disabilities—such as the inability to walk, or to get dressed, without aid—declined from greater than 25 percent in 1982 to less than 20 percent in 1999. And the development of [erectile dysfunction drug] Viagra and vision-correction surgery, among many other drugs and procedures, has allowed many Americans to prolong pleasures historically associated with youth.

Of course, not all the recent improvements in American health and longevity can be directly attributed to our health-care system; some are as much the result of adopting healthier habits (exercise, better diet) or of dropping unhealthy ones (smoking, excessive alcohol consumption). And even though life expectancy has been rising in America, it remains lower than in many other advanced nations—probably because those nations have lower rates of obesity, broader access to health care, and lesser degrees of wealth inequality. Still, better medical care is the principal cause of improvements in American health and life-span over the past fifty years.

## Increase in Health Care Costs

The problem, of course, is that since 1960 health-care spending has grown significantly faster than the economy, meaning that we're spending an ever larger portion of our incomes on medical care. In 1960 health care constituted 5.1 percent of the U.S. economy; in 1980 it constituted 8.8 percent; today [2004] it constitutes 13.3 percent. The Centers for Medicare and Medicaid Services (CMMS) projects that health-care spending will grow by an average of more than seven percent a year until 2012, even after adjusting for inflation. Meanwhile, private health-insurance premiums—which rose by 14 percent last year [2003] alone—are becoming unaffordable for ever more Americans.

It seems that cutting costs should be relatively easy. After all, health-care delivery in the United States is notoriously inefficient. Consumers lack sufficient information or expertise to make informed choices of physicians, hospitals, and treatments. Also, because most of their health care is paid for by insurance, they tend to overuse the system. Physicians, for their part, usually profit from the tests and procedures they order and perform—whether or not those tests and procedures are truly necessary. Shouldn't it be a simple matter to reduce waste and abuse?

Up to a point, yes. The frequency of a major surgical procedure such as coronary bypass surgery varies widely from physician to physician and region to region, with no discernible difference in health outcomes, on average, between patients who receive such treatments and those who don't. According to one study, 20 to 30 percent of health-care spending goes for tests, treatments, and visits that have no positive effect on either the quality or the length of our lives. If we could identify and prevent even half this spending, we would save some $25 billion to $35 billion each year on Medicare alone.

## The Cost of Innovation

But this would do little to address the fundamental problem. That's because the largest driver of growth in health-care spending is not waste or price gouging or the slow aging of the population but, rather, the cost of technological innovation. Even when technological

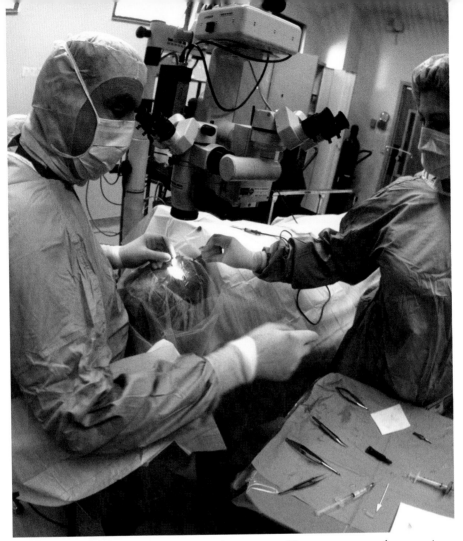

*Even when technological improvements make treatments like cataract surgery less expensive overall, costs often rise because of an increase in the number of the procedures performed.*

improvements make some treatments less expensive and more effective, overall spending often rises. Cataract surgery, for example, used to require up to a week in the hospital and offer only uncertain results. Now it's a quick, highly effective outpatient surgery. Per-procedure costs of this surgery have fallen, on average, by about one percent a year over the long term, after controlling for inflation. But because so many more people opt for cataract surgery today, real total spending on the procedure has risen by four percent a year over the same period. Given the overall growth in health-care spending currently projected by the CMMS, even an immediate drop, through waste reduction, of 20 percent in nationwide spending—which would be

## Higher Health Care Costs Mean More Uninsured

Per capita spending in 2001 dollars.

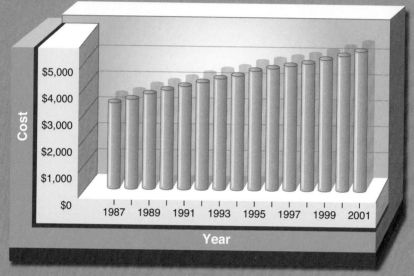

Americans without health insurance, in millions.

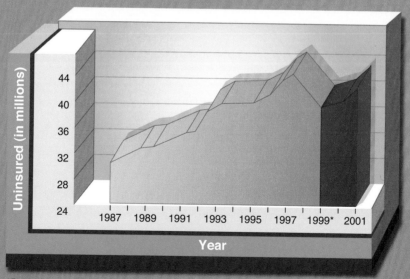

*Beginning with 1999 figures, results reflect a change in Census Bureau question.

Taken from: Don Peck, "Putting a Value on Health," *Atlantic Monthly*, vol. 293, no. 1, Chart Data Sources: *The Wall Street Journal*; Centers for Medicare and Medicaid Services; U.S. Census Bureau.

highly difficult to achieve—would be undone by new technology-fueled spending in just four years.

Most of the growth in health-care spending has produced real improvements in the scope of medical services and the quality of care. But the number of things we can do to cure disease, eliminate discomfort, and stave off aging is expanding faster than the ability of many Americans to pay for them. Indeed, it appears very likely that growth in medical spending will continue to outpace growth in personal income or GDP [gross domestic product] over the next few decades—even if we introduce temporary cost-saving measures.

That we spend enormous sums of money for even tiny improvements in health-care quality reflects a social ethos to which most Americans implicitly subscribe: anything that might improve health or extend life, however marginally, should be made available to everyone, at whatever cost. That may seem morally proper. But because of the way that health care is bought and financed in this country, we tend to be blind to the costs, both economic and moral, of taking this ethos too far. Because neither patients nor physicians pay for them directly, expensive tests, treatments, and procedures of only marginal value are routinely ordered, and expensive new technologies that barely improve the ability to detect or treat a disease are widely and rapidly adopted.

Of course, not every health plan covers every test or treatment, but most health-insurance plans have been rapidly expanding what they cover. The result is a system in which patients with insurance can order up an expensive test that is one percent more effective than a test costing one third as much—indirectly pushing health-care premiums beyond the reach of many others.

## The Issue of Rationing

Is there anything we can do about this? Unfortunately, the most obvious way to significantly reduce health-care costs without substantially decreasing the quality of care is rationing—that is, limiting the range of treatments and tests that insurance will cover in certain circumstances, a practice that runs counter to the prevailing any-care-at-any-cost ethos. Hardly a politician dares even to mouth the word "rationing," save as an expression of opprobrium.

Yet the fact is that the system already rations; we just don't acknowledge it openly. Every day on the front lines and in the back offices of the health-care profession ICU nurses, hospital executives, and Medicare and insurance-company administrators make difficult cost-versus-value decisions. How long should a man in a coma be allowed to linger in an expensive ICU bed while others who could benefit from the specialized care wait? Is it worth $7,000 to give Xigris—a drug to treat virulent infections that can develop in hospital settings—to an uninsured patient with less than three months to live? In a recent survey of 620 critical-care physicians, 68 percent said they had rationed medications or procedures in the preceding year. Such decisions are often morally complex, even agonizing—and often benefit patients with money: overall, people who have health insurance receive about twice as much medical care as those who lack it.

Without intervention this gap will most likely widen: a majority of Americans will continue to receive state-of-the-art care, whereas a growing minority will be shut out of the insurance system, finding themselves without access either to the cutting-edge treatments of 2004 or to proven forms of medical care that have been available for decades.

## EVALUATING THE AUTHORS' ARGUMENTS:

In this viewpoint Peck contends that the cost of technological innovation is the main driver of higher health care costs, whereas in the previous viewpoint, the authors argued that the main source of high cost is third-party employer health coverage. Though they disagree about the main source of high costs, what fact about the way patients use the system do both agree plays a role in driving cost upward?

# The U.S. Health Care System Spends Too Much Money Without Good Health Results

*"The United States spends by far the most on health care per person. . . . Yet we are near the bottom in nearly every measure of our health."*

Doug Pibel and Sarah van Gelder

In the following viewpoint Doug Pibel and Sarah van Gelder contend that the U.S. health care system is broken, suffering from skyrocketing costs, many uninsured or underinsured people, and poor health outcomes. Pibel and van Gelder claim that most people in America want universal health insurance like that seen in many other industrialized nations. The authors believe that much of the high costs of the current system could be eliminated by getting rid of the bureaucracy created by unnecessary features of the current system, such as insurance companies. Pibel is managing editor of *Yes! Magazine*, and Gelder is cofounder and executive editor of *Yes! Magazine*.

Reprinted from "Health Care for All," the Fall 2006 issue of *Yes! Magazine. Yes!* is a nonprofit, ad-free publication that offers positive solutions for creating a just and sustainable world. To subscribe, visit www.yesmagazine.org/subscribe or call (800) 937-4451.

For Joel Segal, it was the day he was kicked out of George Washington Hospital, still on an IV after knee surgery, without insurance, and with $100,000 in medical debt. For Kiki Peppard, it was having to postpone needed surgery until she could find a job with insurance—it took her two years. People all over the United States are waking up to the fact that our system of providing health care is a disaster.

## A Broken System

An estimated 50 million Americans lack medical insurance, and a similar and rapidly growing number are underinsured. The uninsured are excluded from services, charged more for services, and die when medical care could save them—an estimated 18,000 die each year because they lack medical coverage.

But it's not only the uninsured who suffer. Of the more than 1.5 million bankruptcies filed in the U.S. each year, about half are a result of medical bills; of those, three-quarters of filers had health insurance.

Businesses are suffering too. Insurance premiums [the amount of money charged for insurance coverage] increased 73 percent between 2000 and 2005, and per capita costs are expected to keep rising. The National Coalition on Health Care (NCHC) estimates that, without reform, national health care spending will double over the next 10 years. The NCHC is not some fringe advocacy group—its co-chairs are Congressmen Robert D. Ray (R-IA) and Paul G. Rogers (D-FL), and it counts General Electric and Verizon among its members.

Employers who want to offer employee health care benefits can't compete with low-road employers who offer none. Nor can they compete with companies located in countries that offer national health insurance.

The shocking facts about health care in the United States are well known. There's little argument that the system is broken. What's not well known is that the dialogue about fixing the health care system is just as broken.

Among politicians and pundits, a universal, publicly funded system is off the table. But Americans in increasing numbers know what their leaders seem not to—that the United States is the only industrialized nation where such stories as Joel's and Kiki's can happen.

And most Americans know why: the United States leaves the health of its citizens at the mercy of an expensive, patchwork system where some get great care while others get none at all.

The overwhelming majority—75 percent, according to an October 2005 Harris Poll—want what people in other wealthy countries have: the peace of mind of universal health insurance.

## A Wild Experiment?

Which makes the discussion all the stranger. The public debate around universal health care proceeds as if it were a wild, untested experiment—as if the United States would be doing something never done before.

Yet universal health care is in place throughout the industrialized world. In most cases, doctors and hospitals operate as private businesses. But government pays the bills, which reduces paperwork costs to a fraction of the American level. It also cuts out expensive insurance corporations and HMOs [health maintenance organizations], with their multimillion-dollar CEO compensation packages, and billions in profit. Small wonder "single payer" systems can cover their entire populations at half the per capita cost. In the United States, people without insurance may live with debilitating disease or pain, with conditions that prevent them from getting jobs or decent pay, putting many on a permanent poverty track. They have more difficulty managing chronic conditions—only two in five have a regular doctor—leading to poorer health and greater cost.

*Polls show that 75 percent of Americans want universal health care.*

## Problems with the U.S. Health Care System

The uninsured are far more likely to wait to seek treatment for acute problems until they become severe.

Even those who have insurance may not find out until it's too late that exclusions, deductibles [the portion of an insurance claim not covered by insurance], co-payments [a set amount paid by the patient at the time of service], and annual limits leave them bankrupt when a family member gets seriously ill.

In 2005, more than a quarter of insured Americans didn't fill prescriptions, skipped recommended treatment, or didn't see a doctor when sick, according to the Commonwealth Fund's 2005 Biennial Health Insurance Survey.

People stay in jobs they hate—for the insurance. Small business owners are unable to offer insurance coverage for employees or themselves. Large businesses avoid setting up shops in the United States—Toyota just chose to build a plant in Canada to escape the skyrocketing costs of U.S. health care.

All of this adds up to a less healthy society, more families suffering the double whammy of financial and health crises, and more people forced to go on disability.

But the public dialogue proceeds as if little can be done beyond a bit of tinkering around the edges. More involvement by government would create an unwieldy bureaucracy, they say, and surely bankrupt us all. The evidence points to the opposite conclusion.

The United States spends by far the most on health care per person—more than twice as much as Europe, Canada, and Japan which all have some version of national health insurance. Yet we are near the bottom in nearly every measure of our health.

The World Health Organization (WHO) ranks the U.S. health care system 37th of 190 countries, well below most of Europe, and trailing Chile and Costa Rica. The United States does even worse in the WHO rankings of performance on level of health—a stunning 72nd. Life expectancy in the U.S. is shorter than in 27 other countries; the U.S. ties with Hungary, Malta, Poland, and Slovakia for infant mortality—ahead of only Latvia among industrialized nations.

## The Cost of Corporate Bureaucracy

Where is the money going? An estimated 15 cents of each private U.S. health care dollar goes simply to shuffling the paperwork. The administrative costs for our patched-together system of HMOs, insurance companies, pharmaceutical manufacturers, hospitals, and government programs are nearly double those for single-payer Canada. It's not

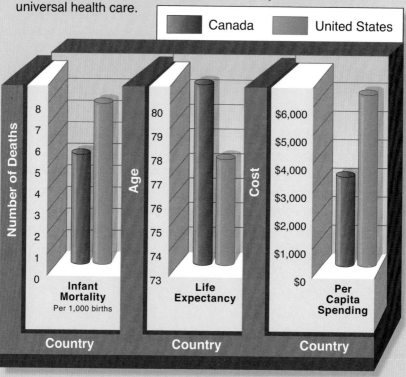

## Side By Side: No Comparison, 2006

Canada and the United States used to be twins on public-health measurements. Here's how it looks after 35 years of Canadian universal health care.

Canada     United States

**Infant Mortality**
Per 1,000 births

Number of Deaths

**Life Expectancy**

Age

**Per Capita Spending**

Cost

Country     Country     Country

Taken from: Holly Dressel, "Has Canada Got the Cure?" *Yes! Magazine*, Fall 2006.

because Americans are inherently less efficient than Canadians—our publicly funded Medicare system spends under five cents per budget dollar on administrative overhead. And the Veterans Administration, which functions like Britain's socialized medical system, spends less per patient but consistently outranks private providers in patient satisfaction and quality of care.

But in the private sector, profits and excessive CEO pay are added to the paperwork and bureaucracy. The U.S. pharmaceutical industry averages a 17 percent profit margin, against three percent for all other businesses. In the health care industry, million-dollar CEO pay packages are the rule, with some executives pulling down more than $30 million a year in salary and amassing billion-dollar stock option packages.

Studies conducted by the General Accounting Office, the Congressional Budget Office, and various states have concluded that a universal, single-payer health care system would cover everyone—including the millions currently without insurance—and still save billions.

Enormous amounts of money are changing hands in the health-industrial complex, but little is going to the front line providers—nurses, nurse practitioners, and home health care workers who put in long shifts for low pay. Many even find they must fight to get access to the very health facilities they serve.

Doctors complain of burnout as patient loads increase. They spend less time with each patient as they spend more time doing insurance company mandated paperwork and arguing with insurance company bureaucrats over treatments and coverage.

In polls, surveys, town meetings, and letters, large majorities of Americans say they have had it with a system that is clearly broken and they are demanding universal health care. Many businesses—despite a distaste for government involvement—are coming to the same view. Doctors, nurses, not-for-profit hospitals, and clinics are joining the call, many specifically saying we need a single-payer system like the system in Canada. And while we hear complaints about Canada's system, a study of 10 years of Canadian opinion polling showed that Canadians are more satisfied with their health care than Americans.

**EVALUATING THE AUTHORS' ARGUMENTS:**

In this viewpoint Pibel and van Gelder agree with the authors of the previous two viewpoints that health care costs are high. Pibel and van Gelder differ with the author of the previous viewpoint, Don Peck, in thinking that the health outcomes of the U.S. health care system are not impressive. Make a list of all of the viewpoints in this chapter and whether they hold similar or different opinions than Pibel and van Gelder.

# Chapter 3

# How Should the Health Care System in America Be Reformed?

*Nancy-Ann De Parle, President Obama's director of the White House Office of Health Care Reform, attends the Iowa White House forum on health care reform. Forums like this are being held across the country.*

# More Government-Provided Care Is Needed to Reform the Health Care System

*"Obama's proposal will modernize our current system of employer- and government-provided health care."*

David M. Cutler, J. Bradford DeLong, and Ann Marie Marciarille

In the following viewpoint David M. Cutler, J. Bradford DeLong, and Ann Marie Marciarille argue that then-candidate Barack Obama's plan for health care system reform, presented during the 2008 presidential campaign, is preferable to the plan presented by his opponent Senator John McCain. The authors argue that government intervention to reform private health care sector as well as government-provided health care will have broad positive impacts on the nation. Cutler is a professor of economics at Harvard, was an adviser to Barack Obama's 2008 presidential campaign, and is the author of *Your Money or Your Life: Strong Medicine for America's*

*Health Care System.* DeLong is a professor of economics at University of California at Berkeley. Marciarille is the AARP Health and Aging Policy Research Fellow at University of the Pacific McGeorge Capital Center for Government Law and Policy.

**AS YOU READ, CONSIDER THE FOLLOWING QUESTIONS:**
1. Under Obama's plan, as the authors describe it, doctors would be rewarded for doing what for Medicare and Medicaid patients?
2. According to the authors, by how much will insurance premiums be lowered for the typical family under Obama's plan?
3. How much more money does the United States spend on health care than Canada and Switzerland, according to the authors?

T he big threat to growth in the next decade is not oil or food prices, but the rising cost of health care. The doubling of health insurance premiums since 2000 makes employers choose between cutting benefits and hiring fewer workers.

Rising health costs push total employment costs up and wages and benefits down. The result is lost profits and lost wages, in addition to pointless risk, insecurity and a flood of personal bankruptcies.

Sustained growth thus requires successful health-care reform. Barack Obama and John McCain [2008 presidential candidates] propose to lead us in opposite directions—and the Obama direction is far superior.

## Five Suggested Reforms

Sen. Obama's proposal will modernize our current system of employer- and government-provided health care, keeping what works well, and making the investments now that will lead to a more efficient medical system. He does this in five ways:

- *Learning.* One-third of medical costs go for services at best ineffective and at worst harmful. Fifty billion dollars will jump-start the long-overdue information revolution in health care to identify the best providers, treatments and patient management strategies.
- *Rewarding.* Doctors and hospitals today are paid for performing procedures, not for helping patients. Insurers make money by dumping

sick patients, not by keeping people healthy. Mr. Obama proposes to base Medicare and Medicaid reimbursements to hospitals and doctors on patient outcomes (lower cholesterol readings, made and kept follow-up appointments) in a coordinated effort to focus the entire payment system around better health, not just more care.

- *Pooling.* The Obama plan would give individuals and small firms the option of joining large insurance pools. With large patient pools, a few people incurring high medical costs will not topple the entire system, so insurers would no longer need to waste time, money and resources weeding out the healthy from the sick, and businesses and individuals would no longer have to subject themselves to that costly and stressful process.
- *Preventing.* In today's health-care market, less than one dollar in 25 goes for prevention, even though preventive services—regular screenings and healthy lifestyle information—are among the most

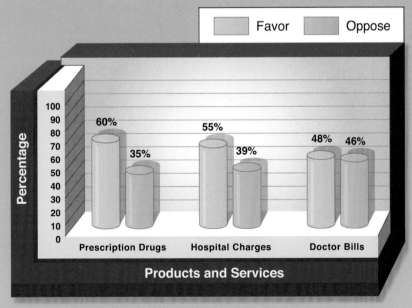

## Favor/Oppose Federal Price Controls

"Would you favor or oppose federal government price controls of the following products and services?"

Favor     Oppose

Prescription Drugs: 60%, 35%
Hospital Charges: 55%, 39%
Doctor Bills: 48%, 46%

Percentage (y-axis: 0 to 100)

Products and Services

Taken from: Harris Interactive, "Most People Think Health Care Costs Are 'Unreasonably High' and Favor Price Controls, According to Harris Poll," The Harris Poll #64, September 9, 2004.

cost-effective medical services around. Guaranteeing access to preventive services will improve health and in many cases save money.

- *Covering.* Controlling long-run health-care costs requires removing the hidden expenses of the uninsured. The reforms described above will lower premiums by $2,500 for the typical family, allowing millions previously priced out of the market to afford insurance.

In addition, tax credits for those still unable to afford private coverage, and the option to buy in to the federal government's benefits system, will ensure that all individuals have access to an affordable, portable alternative at a price they can afford.

## The Impact of Reform

Given the current inefficiencies in our system, the impact of the Obama plan will be profound. Besides the $2,500 savings in medical costs for the typical family, according to our research annual business-sector costs will fall by about $140 billion. Our figures suggest that decreasing employer costs by this amount will result in the expansion of employer-provided health insurance to 10 million previously uninsured people.

We know these savings are attainable: other countries have them today. We spend 40% more than other countries such as Canada and Switzerland on health care—nearly $1 trillion—but our health outcomes are no better.

The lower cost of benefits will allow employers to hire some 90,000 low-wage workers currently without jobs because they are currently priced out of the market. It also would pull one and a half million more workers out of low-wage low-benefit and into high-wage high-benefit jobs. Workers currently locked into jobs because they fear losing their health benefits would be able to move to entrepreneurial jobs, or simply work part time.

> **FAST FACT**
>
> A bill introduced in March 2009, the Preexisting Condition Patient Protection Act, would eliminate preexisting condition exclusions that insurance companies use to deny individuals coverage for preexisting chronic health conditions.

*President Obama speaks to members of Congress about his plans to entertain a wide range of views on how best to reform the world's costliest health care system.*

## A Competing Republican Plan

In contrast, Sen. McCain, who constantly repeats his no-new-taxes promise on the campaign trail, proposes a big tax hike as the solution to our health-care crisis. His plan would raise taxes on workers who receive health benefits, with the idea of encouraging their employers to drop coverage. A study conducted by University of Michigan economist Tom Buchmueller and colleagues published in the journal *Health Affairs* suggests that the McCain tax hike will lead employers to drop coverage for over 20 million Americans.

What would happen to these people? Mr. McCain will give them a small tax credit, $5,000 for a family and $2,500 for an individual, and tell them to navigate the individual insurance market on their own.

For middle- and lower-income people, the credits are way too small. They are less than half the cost of policies today ($12,000 on average for a family), and are far below the 75% that most employers offering coverage contribute. Further, their value would erode over time, as the credit increases less rapidly than average premiums.

Those already sick are completely out of luck, as individual insurers are free to deny coverage due to pre-existing conditions. Mr. McCain has proposed a high-risk pool for the very sick, but has not put forward the money to make it work.

Even for those healthy enough to gain coverage in the individual insurance market, the screening, marketing and individual underwriting that insurers do to separate healthy from sick boosts premiums by 17% relative to employer-provided insurance, well beyond the help offered by the McCain tax credit.

The immediate consequences of the McCain plan are even worse. The McCain plan is a big tax increase on employers and workers. With the economy in recession, that's the last thing America's businesses need.

Finally, Mr. McCain does nothing to bend the curve of rising health-care costs downward. He does not fund investments in learning, rewarding and preventing. Eliminating state coverage requirements will slash preventive service availability.

The high cost-sharing plans he envisions will similarly discourage preventive care. And as he does nothing about the hidden costs of the uncovered—expensive ER visits, recurring conditions resulting from inadequate follow-up care.

Everyone agrees our health-care financing system must change. But only one candidate, Barack Obama, has real change we can believe in.

## EVALUATING THE AUTHORS' ARGUMENTS:

In this viewpoint Cutler, DeLong, and Marciarille argue that Barack Obama's plan for health reform is preferable to John McCain's plan. As the authors describe the different plans, identify two key differences between Obama's plan and McCain's plan.

# Less Government-Provided Care Is Needed to Reform the Health Care System

**Dave Camp**

*"We are promoting an American solution to drive down costs and give everyone access to quality, affordable health care."*

In the following viewpoint Dave Camp argues that the Democrats' plan for health care reform relies on too much government-provided health care. The Republican alternative, Camp maintains, provides better results by not relying on government-provided health care. Camp claims that tax benefits, the ability to purchase health insurance without constraints, using technology, and focusing on prevention are the key components to health care reform. Camp is a congressman in the U.S. House of Representatives for Michigan's fourth congressional district.

**AS YOU READ, CONSIDER THE FOLLOWING QUESTIONS:**

1. What three things does the Democrats' plan for health care do similarly to western Europe and Canada, according to Camp?

Dave Camp, "Health Care by Uncle Sam: There Is a Better Way than HillaryCare 2.0," *The Washington Times,* July 29, 2008. Reproduced by permission.

2. What percentage of Americans get health insurance through their employer, according to the author?
3. According to Camp, how many deaths are caused every year by preventable medical errors?

Nov. 20, 1993. That is when "HillaryCare" was introduced in the House of Representatives. Today, the Democrats, including presumptive Democratic presidential nominee Barack Obama, are still pushing for a government takeover of health care. Call it HillaryCare 2.0. Call it Medicare for All. Call it whatever you want, but it still puts the federal government at the center of your health care.

The rhetoric has improved, but the policy has not. It still requires a massive increase in taxes that we cannot afford. It rations care, limits choices and limits procedures just as it has in Western Europe and in Canada. No wonder we said "no" 15 years ago.

Even our northern neighbors are recognizing this mistake. The founder of the Canadian system, Claude Castonguay, was recently quoted saying: "We thought we could resolve the system's problems by rationing services or injecting massive amounts of new money into it." Now, however, he says they are "proposing to give a greater role to the private sector so that people can exercise freedom of choice."

Republicans are offering a better alternative. Instead of looking abroad for healthcare solutions, we are promoting an American solution to drive down costs and give everyone access to quality, affordable health care.

We do that by 1) leveling the playing field so every American gets a tax benefit to purchase health care, just like businesses do; 2) eliminating legal and regulatory barriers that drive up costs; 3) utilizing technology to save lives and money; and, 4) focusing on prevention and wellness, not just treating you once you are already sick.

How does it work? First, we will lower costs and let you keep your insurance if you change or lose your job by using the power of the tax code. The tax code created employer-provided health care and it is time for the tax code to create personal, individual health care.

Nearly 85 percent of Americans who have health insurance get it through their employer. That's because since World War II we have provided companies with a tax incentive to do so.

*The author cites the founder of Canada's health care system Claude Castonguay's admission of problems in the Canadian system and proposals to give the private sector a greater role as proof that government-run health care does not work.*

# Drug Companies Take Advantage of U.S. Consumers

| Drug | Use | U.S. | Canada | Markup to U.S. Consumers |
|------|-----|------|--------|--------------------------|
| Lipitor | Cholesterol | $321.30 | $164.34 | 96% |
| Plavix | Cardiovascular Disease | $370.41 | $252.90 | 46% |
| Prevacid | Ulcers | $419.96 | $213.36 | 97% |
| Zocor | Cholesterol | $178.87 | $136.98 | 31% |
| Nexium | Acid Reflux | $417.48 | $269.10 | 55% |
| Zoloft | Depression | $248.81 | $163.83 | 52% |
| Zyprexa | Depression | $556.54 | $244.56 | 128% |
| Neurontin | Seizures | $147.65 | $102.60 | 44% |
| Effexor XR | Depression | $302.18 | $169.20 | 79% |
| Advair Diskus | Asthma | $157.37 | $85.02 | 85% |

Taken from: Byron Dorgan, "Reducing Cost of Prescription Drugs," www.dorgan.senate.gov, March 3, 2007.

While we must protect employer-provided health care, the generosity of the American taxpayers should not go to businesses alone. Tax incentives to purchase and save for health insurance should apply to individuals, small businesses and large corporations alike.

Second, we will further reduce costs by letting you shop around. No more unnecessary and redundant regulatory and legal barriers that limit your options and limit the services offered by local doctors and hospitals.

If you can go on the Internet and shop for the best deal on a washer and dryer, a car, a home, a mortgage or life insurance, then you should be able to do the same for health insurance.

Someone's health in Michigan is not so different from someone in Ohio. But in America you can't buy health insurance from a provider in a neighboring state, let alone across the country. This is wrong and we should eliminate these artificial barriers.

And, you should know what you are paying for. By creating greater transparency you will be able to go online to find reviews for your doctor and your hospital the same way you would for any other product. The technology is there, the data is there, and we should be able to access it. No more hiding the fact that you or your insurance are being billed $15 for a pill that only costs 35 cents!

Third, we must realize the revolution in technology and the Internet aren't just for Silicon Valley and manufacturers. Utilized by hospitals and patients alike these tools—like e-records, e-prescribing and quality information—will also save lives and money.

There are nearly 100,000 deaths caused every year by preventable medical errors. Health information technology can literally save tens of thousands of Americans every year. And, by eliminating duplicative procedures and clerical mistakes we will save a minimum of $81 billion annually, enough to reduce out-of-pocket expenses for a family by 25 percent.

Fourth, we apply the wisdom of Benjamin Franklin's adage that an ounce of prevention is worth a pound of cure—that simple fact is truer in health care than anywhere else. When we start paying for cholesterol medication instead of heart attacks, we will not only save lives, we will save money. Wellness must be a focal point of our health-care system.

Armed with the same tax benefits larger employers use to provide health-care coverage, along with regulatory reforms, a focus on prevention and wellness, and the use of technology, we will unleash the power of individuals and small businesses to purchase quality health care.

There is an alternative to government owned and operated health care, and Republicans are providing it.

## EVALUATING THE AUTHORS' ARGUMENTS:

In this viewpoint Camp identifies four key components of the Republican proposal for health care reform. Comparing these with the five components of Obama's Democratic proposal in the previous viewpoint, identify at least one similarity and one difference.

# A Consumer-Driven Health Care System Is the Best System

**Bill Steigerwald, interviewing Regina Herzlinger**

*"[In] a consumer-driven system ... you and I would be buying the health insurance."*

In the following viewpoint Bill Steigerwald interviews Regina Herzlinger, who argues that what the U.S. health care system needs is reform to make it consumer driven. Herzlinger argues that neither government nor businesses should be the ones providing health care to U.S. citizens—rather, individuals should be shopping for their own health insurance in a market that allows choice. Steigerwald is associate editor at the *Pittsburgh Tribune-Review*. Herzlinger is the Nancy R. McPherson Professor of Business Administration Chair at the Harvard Business School, senior fellow at the Manhattan Institute Center for Medical Progress, and the author of *Who Killed Health Care?* and *Consumer-Driven Health Care: Implications for Providers, Payers, and Policymakers*.

Bill Steigerwald, interviewing Regina Herzlinger, "Health Care & Its Cure," *Pittsburgh Tribune-Review*, February 16, 2008. Reproduced by permission.

1. What does Herzlinger identify as the essential problem with the current health care system?
2. What does Herzlinger dislike about then-presidential candidate Hillary Clinton's health care plan?
3. In what way does Herzlinger believe that we are headed in the right direction with health care?

*M*oney magazine has dubbed Regina Herzlinger the "Godmother" of consumer-driven health care, and it's not just because she has written books with titles like "Consumer-Driven Health Care: Implications for Providers, Payers and Policymakers." The first woman to be "tenured and chaired" at Harvard Business School, Professor Herzlinger is widely known for her innovative research into health care. Her latest book is last year's "Who Killed Health Care?" It outlines her plan for creating a consumer-driven system that would deliver affordable, high-quality care to everyone by putting insurance money in the hands of patients, removing the third-party middleman in the doctor-patient relationship and giving employers cost relief. I talked to Herzlinger Wednesday by phone from her office in Cambridge, Mass.:

*Q: What is your shorthand description of the health-care system we have now in the United States?*

**A:** Too costly and too erratic in quality, but still a system that preserves people's choice.

*Q: What do you mean by "still preserves people's choice"?*

**A:** You're not forced to go with a single-payer system where you have no independent voice about what you'll pay for what kinds of benefits.

*Q: Is our health-care system as bad as our politicians and the media tell us it is?*

**A:** Well, not all the politicians think it's that bad, but certainly the media trumpets that—and it is a hugely unfair kind of trumpeting. One of the issues is that the World Health Organization ranks us as very low in quality of care. Of course, one of its criteria for quality of care is whether everybody is insured or not. That seems like not a

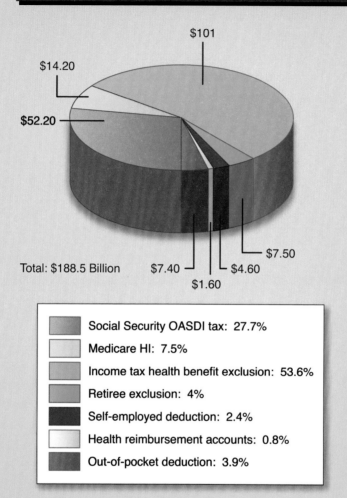

## Federal Tax Expenditures for Health Insurance (in Billions)

$101

$14.20

$52.20

Total: $188.5 Billion    $7.40    $4.60    $7.50

$1.60

Social Security OASDI tax: 27.7%

Medicare HI: 7.5%

Income tax health benefit exclusion: 53.6%

Retiree exclusion: 4%

Self-employed deduction: 2.4%

Health reimbursement accounts: 0.8%

Out-of-pocket deduction: 3.9%

Taken from: Nina Owcharenko, "Health Care Tax Credits: Designing an Alternative to Employer-Based Coverage," Backgrounder #1895, Heritage Foundation, November 8, 2005.

good criterion to use. Most of the important research in medicine, which is so promising to finally make medicine into a real science, is done in the U.S. And certainly, if you compare the U.S. to a country like Japan or Germany or the Scandinavian countries, it's a ridiculous comparison because if you go to Japan or Germany you won't see the diversity we have in the United States. And certain ancestries are much more prone to certain kinds of illnesses than others. For example, African-Americans are much more prone to cardiovascular disease and diabetes than Caucasians. So this kind of willy-nilly quality measure that doesn't adjust for the differences within the population seems to me ridiculous.

*Q: Who are the bad guys who are wrecking or ruining or distorting our health-care system?*

**A:** Well, essentially the problem is that you and I have taken part of our salaries and given them to our employers to use in buying health insurance on our behalf. There is no way they could buy our clothes or our homes or anything else as well as we can—and they don't do a very good job of buying health insurance, either. The only reason we've done that is because they can use our salaries pre-tax to buy health insurance, whereas if I were cashed out by Harvard and it gave me back the $15,000 I use on health care, I would have to pay taxes on those $15,000; I could only use after-tax money. So as inept as employers are in buying health insurance for their employees—and they are inept not because they are stupid but because how can they possibly know what you want versus what I want; we only do it because of the tax status, and that's a big problem.

The same problem—i.e., a third party buying on our behalf—also holds for Medicare, where the purchasing is done by the U.S. government, and for Medicaid, where the purchasing is done by state and local governments. So the biggest problem with our health-care system is that the agents we have appointed to take care of health insurance and health care—which are the government and businesses—are not very good at it.

*Q: If we had a consumer-driven system of health care, what would it look like?*

**A:** Everybody would be required to buy health insurance. If you were poor, you wouldn't be stuffed into Medicaid, which is not a great program because lots of doctors refuse to see Medicaid patients because they get paid so badly for them. Instead, you would be given money to go out and shop for health insurance just like everybody else. Eventually, people on Medicare would be cast out and they could buy what they wanted. That's what a consumer-driven system would look like—in other words, you and I would be buying the health insurance.

The second crucial attribute of this system is in order to make sure that we weren't buying stupid, we would need a lot of information, not only about the quality of our health insurers but also about the quality of the health-care providers that they provide access to. I need open-heart surgery? How good is this doctor in that hospital versus another doctor in some other kind of hospital?

That's what we need.

*Q: What or who is the chief obstacle to our developing a better system?*

**A:** One is this tax preference, where only your employer can use pre-tax money to buy health insurance; that's a huge barrier and it's a big (undertaking) for employers. They don't like buying insurance; they have a business to run. They have a paper to publish or something else to do and they are obligated to buy this very important item for us. So the tax preference is a huge item and Democrat or Republican, that will be corrected by the next president. The problem that is much more difficult to correct is the problem of transparency, and that is that providers do not want to be measured and they are hugely powerful. But unless we know whether we are buying a Toyota or an Edsel, we're never going to get to a higher-quality, lower-cost health-care system. And the only way you and I can know that, because we are not doctors and we are not scientists, is if we had good data that was accessible to us.

*Q: The same kind of data we have when we buy a car?*

**A:** Or a computer. Nobody understands how they work. Nevertheless, computers have become cheaper and better and they have become consumer items because there's terrific information. That's why Dell, for example, flourished because people like me who don't know a bit from a byte nevertheless knew Dell was a good purveyor. It no longer is, but when I first bought a computer it was a good purveyor.

*Q: What do you think of Hillary Clinton's health-care plan?*

**A:** Well, I like the universal coverage and she does have choice, so allegedly under her plan you could choose to either buy a private health insurance or a public insurance. That's the rub. The public choice that she would offer is hugely subsidized. For instance, she would offer Medicare for people like us. Well, Medicare—ha—for every eight dollars spent, seven dollars are paid by somebody other than the recipient. So if we were offered Medicare, which is hugely subsidized, of course we would opt for it. But we would put a tremendous burden on our children and grandchildren, and we would enlarge the government's stranglehold on the health-care system. Government is not good for health care. Government is political.

Government is bureaucratic. Government kills off innovation. Not a good idea. Her plans for controlling costs are equally bureaucratic. It is that the government would tell doctors how to practice medicine better. Already, physicians in their 50s and 60s can't wait to leave the profession. They just can't stand it. This would put the final nails in the physician coffins.

*Q: Does any politician have a better plan than Mrs. Clinton?*

**A:** I think McCain has a pretty good plan. He's very high on transparency. None of the other candidates really push transparency because the special interests are so powerful and they don't want it. McCain has the courage to say, "I'm going to make data available about how good your doctors and hospitals are," so in that way it's better. Both Mrs. Clinton and McCain advocate something else that's very important, and that is they want to get away from "pricing by procedures," where a doctor makes money only when he does something for you. That might seem like a good way to price, but what it stops doctors from doing is doing things that might make you a lot healthier, because if they make you a lot healthier, the doctor won't be paid anymore. This is called "procedure-based pricing" and it's very pernicious. It stops providers from making sure that they catch diseases early on, for example, or that they use less-costly interventions because although doctors are very good human beings, they are also financial human beings, so they get a financial benefit for doing more rather than a financial benefit for making us healthier so we don't need them so much. Both Clinton and McCain understand this and have promised to change this form of pricing.

> **FAST FACT**
>
> Switzerland has a consumer-driven health care system that requires all residents to purchase health insurance among many public and private insurance companies, and subsidizes low-income individuals.

*Q: Are we heading in the right or wrong direction on health care?*

**A:** I think we're headed toward universal coverage, which I think is a very good idea for the simple reason that if you're sick, the 20

*Harvard Business School professor and author Regina Herzlinger is widely known in academic circles for her innovative research into consumer-driven health care.*

percent of the people who are sick spend 80 percent of the money on health care. If you are sick and uninsured, there's no way you will be able to get health insurance because it is so expensive. So until we have the healthy subsidizing the sick, the sick in the United States who don't have health insurance are going to be in the terrible situation of being both sick and uninsured.

McCain doesn't like universal coverage. Neither does Obama. Only Mrs. Clinton is for it. However, Mrs. Clinton and Obama are both for a lot of government intervention. In health care, that's a really bad thing. McCain is the only one who wants everything to be done through the private sector. For example, he would subsidize people so they could go out and buy health insurance rather than having the government dictate the insurance policy to them.

*Q: Like food stamps?*

**A:** Like food stamps. Correct.

*Q: Are you optimistic or pessimistic that our political leaders have the wisdom to take their paws off health care and allow a free market or a semblance of one to develop?*

**A:** No. If the Democrats get elected, absolutely not. And what I now see, they are all about more government—more government funding, more government control. I teach at the Harvard Business School. In a class of 100 students, I have 20 fully trained doctors. I say, "What the heck are you doing here? Why aren't you practicing medicine?" They say, "I cannot practice medicine any more." That's a tragedy and that tragedy will become much worse under a Democratic administration.

## EVALUATING THE AUTHOR'S ARGUMENTS:

In this viewpoint Herzlinger explains why she believes a consumer-driven health care system would work best to achieve the goal of universal coverage. What is a possible barrier to universal coverage under this plan?

# A Consumer-Driven Health Care System Is Not the Best System

*"Consumer-driven plans just postpone the question of affordability. The wealthy can always afford their care. Poor people can't."*

**Trudy Lieberman, interviewing Timothy Jost**

In the following viewpoint Trudy Lieberman interviews Timothy Jost, who argues that consumer-driven health care is not the preferable way to deliver health care. Jost contends that consumer-driven health care will favor the wealthy and harm the poor. In addition, Jost denies the claim made by proponents of the system that consumer-driven health care would lead to lower health care costs. Lieberman directs the health and medical reporting program in the graduate school of journalism at City University of New York and is a contributing editor to the *Columbia Journalism Review*. Jost is a law professor at Washington and Lee University and author of *Health Care at Risk: A Critique of the Consumer-Driven Movement*.

Trudy Lieberman, "Excluded Voices: An Interview with Timothy Jost," *Columbia Journalism Review*, February 9, 2009. Reproduced by permission of the publisher and the author.

**AS YOU READ, CONSIDER THE FOLLOWING QUESTIONS:**

1. As Jost explains it, what is an HSA?
2. Are the healthy or the unhealthy more likely to sign up for consumer-driven plans, according to the author?
3. According to Jost, how do consumer-driven health plans change the relationship between doctor and patient?

*T*he Washington Post recently [January 25, 2009] ran an utterly predictable and formulaic story about consumer driven health plans—those newfangled options that come with tax-advantaged savings accounts, and are, some would say, the future of American health insurance. Basically, policyholders shoulder more of their health care costs, relieving insurance companies from as much of the claims burden as possible. After getting beyond the requisite anecdotal lead, about a woman who is facing "steep increases in out-of-pocket expenses for health coverage this year," we learn that employers are planning to shove more costs onto their workers. The consulting firm, Mercer, surveyed almost 2,000 large employers and found that 44 percent planned to make workers pay a higher portion of their health insurance premiums this year, up from 40 percent in 2008. Higher premiums often lead workers to clamor for lower deductibles [an insurance clause that specifies an initial amount paid by the patient, after which the insurance company will pay]. So there's a need to understand just how these high deductible offerings work. To that end, Campaign Desk talked to comsumer-driven health plan expert Timothy Jost, law professor at Washington and Lee University and author of *Health Care at Risk: A Critique of the Consumer-Driven Movement*, published in 2007.

## Consumer-Driven Health Care

*Trudy Lieberman: What do we mean by consumer-driven health plans?*

Timothy Jost: It's an imprecise term that means different things to different people. But at its core, it means an arrangement that transfers to consumers much of the responsibility for buying their own health care, just as they would buy cars or computers.

*How do the kinds of consumer-driven policies differ?*

Health savings accounts, or HSAs, are savings accounts to which consumers or their employers can make tax-advantaged contributions. HSAs must be coupled with a high deductible insurance policy; in other words, a plan that covers catastrophic expenses. Consumers can use the money in the account to pay for medical bills they incur before they meet their deductible. Health reimbursement accounts, or HRAs, also come with a savings account, but only employers can make contributions. HRAs are usually linked to a high deductible policy, but they don't have to be.

Balances in the HSA and HRA savings accounts can be rolled over from year to year. If you have an HSA and leave the job, you can take your money with you. If you have an HRA, the money usually stays with the employer.

*Are employers putting money into HSAs?*

A lot of employers are providing high deductible policies. Some are contributing to the HSAs, and some are not. A study by the Blue Cross Blue Shield Association found that only 38 percent of consumers with HSAs received contributions from their employers in 2008, down from 45 percent in 2007. Other research shows that millions of Americans have high deductible plans, but no health savings accounts to help them pay for care while they are meeting the deductible.

## The High Deductibles

*How high do these deductibles go?*

The latest report from the Kaiser Family Foundation and the Health Research and Education Trust found that the average family deductible for HSAs offered by employers was almost $4,000. Deductibles for policies with an HRA can be much higher, and sometimes are. But under the law, deductibles for tax-subsidized HSAs can not exceed the maximum amount a person has to pay out-of-pocket, which is $5,800 for individuals and $11,600 for families.

*What's the rationale behind these high deductibles?*

Supporters believe that when consumers have to spend their own money, they will think twice before running off to the doctor. And when they do, they will shop for the doctor who will offer the best price and quality, much the way they shop for a TV set. They also

*President Bush was an early proponent of health savings accounts and participated in a panel discussion in April 2006 on the subject.*

argue that the high deductibles will cause the price of care to come down because these policies will offer skimpier coverage and consumers will use fewer services which, of course, keeps premiums [price of insurance] down.

*Has that happened?*

Insurers say yes, but we really don't know. There is evidence that people with HSAs from their employers are more likely to participate in exercise, stress management, and nutrition programs. They are also more likely to seek out health information and keep track of their health care expenses. They are healthier and use fewer medical services. Advocates of these plans believe that people in consumer-driven plans spend less money, and their employers save money. But an employer's insurance premium may just be lower because employers are simply shifting costs to their workers. One study showed that, on the surface, these plans saved employers a lot of money. But when you look harder at the data, you see that the savings were largely attributable to healthier workers signing up for the consumer-driven plans, leaving the less healthy workers in more traditional plans.

## The Consumer

*Can consumers really bargain with doctors for cheaper services?*

It's silly to believe that consumers bargaining with doctors and hospitals can bring down costs. It makes no sense. Even the insurers don't believe that. It's not going to happen. Consumers aren't going to the hospital to drive a hard bargain. Medicare and insurance companies will always get a better deal.

*Is it reasonable to expect that consumers can bring down health care costs?*

Relying on consumers to put the brakes on costs is problematic. The information is not there to allow them to do that, and if it were, consumers often would not be in a position to rationally process information. Successful cost control is much more likely to come from the government, or private payers saying that they are not going to pay for medical products and services that don't work.

*Have consumer-driven policies hurt people's health?*

People in high deductible plans have a harder time getting care. They are more likely not to fill prescriptions or go to the doctor, and less likely to get the health care they need. A study by the RAND Corp. showed that consumers could not discriminate between nonessential care and necessary care, and they basically saved money by not going to the doctor.

## Concerns About Consumer-Driven Care

*Do HSAs further health care equity?*

No. HSAs definitely favor wealthier people. There's pretty good evidence that where people have an option of an HSA plan, HSA plans are chosen more by wealthier employees. . . . These plans protect neither the health nor financial security of people who are poor.

*Do they further a two-tier health care system?*

More wealthy people use these plans; they get tax benefits and generous contributions to their HSAs. Lower income workers get high deductibles. That means health insurance may be affordable, but when you get sick, health care is not. Just because insurance is affordable doesn't mean that someone can get affordable care. Consumer-driven plans just postpone the question of affordability. The wealthy can always afford their care. Poor people can't.

*How do these plans affect the doctor-patient relationship?*

The relationship between the patient and physician has traditionally been viewed as one of trust. Patients entrust themselves to their doctors, who have an obligation to put the patients' interests first. At least, that's the ideal. The vision for consumer-driven health plans assumes that the physician and other care providers are merchants and patients are consumers. So let the buyer beware. This change threatens the welfare of patients who now cannot trust their doctors to look after their medical needs. Trust is an important aspect of healing. If you approach your doctor as you would a used car dealer, he or she probably won't be able to help you as much.

*What legal issues do these plans raise?*

They raise a host of legal issues that we have not even begun to sort out. Does the duty of a doctor to secure informed consent to treatment now include an obligation to provide information about cost as well as risks and benefits? Might a doctor who withholds medically necessary care because a patient cannot afford to cover deductibles, coinsurance, and copayments be liable for malpractice . . . Do state managed care bills of rights apply to insurers when they are deciding whether or not the cost of a service counts against a deductible? Are there any limits on how much a provider can charge a patient who is paying for a service out-of-pocket if both have not agreed on a price beforehand? (They almost never do.) Are insurers liable to patients or providers if they provide incorrect information in their quality rankings?

## The Future of Consumer-Driven Care

*How important are these plans in the so-called individual market, where people have to assume the entire cost of the policy?*

# It Is the Highest in the World

U.S. public per capita spending covering 26 percent of the population is higher than public spending for universal health care in Europe, Canada, and Australia.

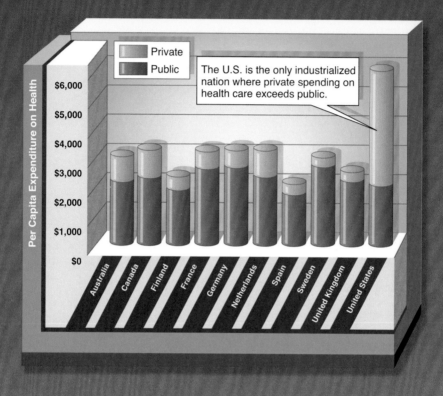

The U.S. is the only industrialized nation where private spending on health care exceeds public.

Taken from: Lilja Otto, "Just the Facts," *Yes!*, Fall 2006. World Health Organization, World Health Report 2005.

They will take over an even larger part of the individual and small group market if nothing is done to reform health care. They won't be very important if [President Barack] Obama is successful in creating a public plan, like Medicare, that people can join. If that happens, nobody in his or her right mind would choose a high deductible plan if they can buy a comprehensive and cheaper policy through a public plan.

*How will this dynamic threaten sellers of these plans in the context of health reform?*

If Congress can pass legislation offering Americans affordable care with reasonable cost-sharing, I would not expect Americans to choose consumer-driven plans instead of a public option.

*How robust is this market in general?*

Both the employer and the individual have grown significantly since 2003, when these plans were first authorized on a large scale. But there are signs that growth has leveled off. Whether the market will continue to grow depends a lot on whether health reform is adopted and whether there will be a public plan. That will be a major sticking point in reform.

## EVALUATING THE AUTHORS' ARGUMENTS:

In this viewpoint Jost contends that no one would choose a high-deductible consumer-driven health care plan over a public plan. What would Regina Herzlinger, proponent of consumer-driven health care in the previous viewpoint, say about Jost's claim?

Viewpoint

5

*"An expanded and improved Medicare for All (Medicare 2.0) program would cover everyone comprehensively within our current expenditures and eliminate the need for private insurance."*

# A Single-Payer System Is the Preferable Health Care System

## Leonard Rodberg and Don McCanne

In the following viewpoint Leonard Rodberg and Don McCanne argue that the United States should adopt a single-payer health care system, in which health care providers are paid from one source of money, thus replacing health insurance providers with one nonprofit or public health care payer. Rodberg and McCanne claim that private health insurance worked when health care costs were much lower, but today even the average family cannot afford health care with private insurance. Rodberg is associate professor and department chair of the Urban Studies Department at Queens College of the City University of New York. McCanne is a physician and a senior health policy fellow at Physicians for a National Health Program (PNHP), where he writes a daily health policy update.

Leonard Rodberg and Don McCanne, "Upgrading to National Health Insurance (Medicare 2.0): The Case for Eliminating Obsolete Private Health Insurance," CommonDreams.org, July 13, 2007. Reproduced by permission.

**AS YOU READ, CONSIDER THE FOLLOWING QUESTIONS:**
1. According to the authors, a private health insurance premium averages how much money for an individual per year?
2. Rodberg and McCanne claim that health insurance premiums rose how much in the six years prior to 2007, when they wrote this piece?
3. The authors claim that how much money in wasteful expenditures could be saved by adopting a single nonprofit or public fund for health care?

P rivate health insurance was an idea that worked during part of the last century; it will not succeed through the 21st Century. With jobs increasingly service-based and short-term, the large employment-based risk pools that made this insurance system possible no longer exist. Medical care has become more effective and more essential to the ordinary person, but also more costly and capital-intensive. *The multiple private insurance carriers that emerged during the last century can no longer provide a sound basis for financing our modern health care system.*

## Private Insurance Today

Alone among the nations of the world, the U.S. has relied upon private insurance to cover the majority of its population. In the mid-20th Century, when medical care accounted for barely 1% of our gross national product, medical technology was limited, and jobs lasted for a lifetime, health care could be financed through such employment-based, premium-financed [the cost of insurance] health insurance. But the time for private insurance has passed.

Health care has now become a major part of our national expenditures. The premium for an individual now averages more than $4,000 per year, while a good family policy averages more than $10,000 per year, comparable to the minimum wage and nearly one-fourth of the median family income. As a consequence, though the US spends far more on health care than any other nation, we leave millions of our people without any coverage at all. And those who do have coverage increasingly find that their plans are inadequate, exposing them to financial hardship and even bankruptcy when illness strikes.

"Health Care/Wealth Care," cartoon by Ed Fischer. Copyright © Ed Fischer. Reproduction rights obtainable from www.CartoonStock.com.

If we believe that everyone should have health care coverage, and that financial barriers should not prevent us from accessing health care when we need it, then it has become clear that the private health insurance system cannot meet our needs. Health care has simply become too expensive to be financed through private insurance premiums.

## Support for Private Insurance

Supporters of insurance companies claim that they create efficiency through competition. However, the truth is that insurance industry is increasingly concentrated, with three national firms, United Health, Wellpoint, and Aetna, dominating the industry. And the high and rising cost of health care shows that whatever competition there was in the past has not worked to hold down costs.

Supporters of private insurance also claim that it expands consumer choice. However, the choice of plans that these companies offer is not what consumers want; it is the choice of their physician and hospital, exactly the choice that private insurance plans, in the guise of managed care, increasingly deny us.

What has been the response of the health insurance industry to this situation? To protect their markets and try to make premiums affordable, they have reduced the protection afforded by insurance by shifting more of the cost to patients, especially through high-deductible [the initial amount of patient must pay before the insurance company will pay a medical claim] plans. They have also targeted their marketing more narrowly to the healthy portion of the population, so as to avoid covering individuals with known needs for health care. Yet premiums continue to rise each year, increasing by nearly 70% above inflation in just the last six years.

The so-called "universal health care" proposals being put forward by mainstream politicians would simply expand the current system without addressing any of its problems. They would simply mandate that either our employers provide us with coverage or we, as individuals, purchase our own coverage in the private insurance market. *These plans cannot work in the face of the high cost of premium-based coverage for even the average person.* (Some proposals would offer the option of buying a competing public plan, under the theory that the public program would be more efficient and effective. The flaw here is that the public plan would attract those who are unable to afford private coverage or who are paying high premiums or have no insurance because of pre-existing conditions. Placing these high-cost individuals in a separate government pool would make it unaffordable for most other people. This "death spiral" would cause the public plan to fail.)

**FAST FACT**

Among countries in the world that have single-payer health insurance programs are Australia, Canada, Finland, France, New Zealand, Sweden, and the United Kingdom.

## Unaffordable for Most

The main impetus [driving force] for renewed interest in health care reform has been the rapid rise in costs over the last few years. Yet, while most of these proposals give lip service to the need to control costs, none actually addresses the problem in a serious way. (The introduction of health information technology and "disease management,"

*Nurses and health care activists rally in support of single-payer health care in Los Angeles on April 6, 2009.*

which some of them urge, are mere placebos; they may make politicians feel better, but studies have shown they will do little to reduce costs and may actually increase them.)

Everyone acknowledges that coverage for low-income individuals must be subsidized [offset by financial government assistance]. But what about the average-income individual and family? If they must now be subsidized as well, we might as well throw in the towel and recognize that a more efficient, more equitable financing system has to be adopted if it has any chance of providing coverage while being affordable to the society. An individual mandate to purchase private insurance cannot provide good coverage while remaining affordable, while employer-provided coverage also can no longer be sustained as the premium costs to the employer become increasingly unaffordable.

## A Single Payer

The private insurance industry spends about 20 percent of its revenue on administration, marketing, and profits. Further, this industry imposes on physicians and hospitals an administrative burden in billing and insurance-related functions that consumes another 12 percent of insurance premiums. Thus, about one-third of private insurance premiums are absorbed in administrative services that could be drastically reduced if we were to finance health care through a single non-profit or public fund. Indeed, studies have shown that replacing the multiplicity of public and private payers with a single national health insurance program would eliminate $350 billion in wasteful expenditures, enough to pay for the care that the uninsured and the underinsured are not currently receiving.

Such a single payer plan would make possible a set of mechanisms, including public budgeting and investment planning, that would allow us to address the real sources of cost increases and allow us to rationalize our health care investments. The drivers of high cost such as administrative waste, deterioration of our primary care infrastructure, excessive prices, and use of non-beneficial or detrimental high-tech services and products could all be addressed within such a rationalized system.

In sum, we will not be able to control health care costs until we reform our method of financing health care. *We simply have to give up the fantasy that the private insurance industry can provide us with comprehensive coverage when this requires premiums that average-income individuals cannot afford.* Instead, the U.S. already has a successful program that covers more than forty million people, gives free choice of doctors and hospitals, and has only three percent administrative expense. It is Medicare, and an expanded and improved Medicare for All (Medicare 2.0) program would cover everyone comprehensively within our current expenditures and eliminate the need for private insurance. This is the direction we must go.

**Viewpoint**

**6**

## A Single-Payer System Is Not the Preferable Health Care System

### Kevin C. Fleming

*"The evidence-based approach to health policy finds little to support the promised superiority of national health insurance."*

In the following viewpoint Kevin C. Fleming argues that a single-payer health care system, in which insurance companies are replaced by one national system, should be avoided. Fleming raises concerns that proponents of the system are not looking hard enough at the evidence, and he points to what he views as several ill effects of adopting a single-payer health care system, with evidence from countries that have such a system. Fleming claims that a single-payer health care system will lead overall to reduced quality, high costs, and a loss of choice. Fleming is assistant professor of medicine and neurology and an internist in the general internal medicine division at the Mayo Clinic in Rochester, Minnesota.

Kevin C. Fleming, "High-Priced Pain: What to Expect from a Single-Payer Health Care System," *Backgrounder*, September 22, 2006. Reproduced by permission.

AS YOU READ, CONSIDER THE FOLLOWING QUESTIONS:
  1. Fleming claims that the proponents of a single-payer health care system have what "ideological vision" of the system?
  2. According to Fleming, how many patients in Britain, under their national health system, are waiting for hospital care?
  3. Why are investments in medical technology slower under a single-payer health care system, according to the author?

There is renewed interest in "socialized medicine." Some prominent Americans want the United States to adopt national health insurance as a means to cover the uninsured, to establish equality of care, and to control health care costs. Their preferred method is a single-payer health care system in which the government, through taxation, finances and regulates the delivery of health care services.

## Ideology over Experience

In fact, the single-payer solution to the problem of the uninsured is a "nirvana approach" to health care. Proponents often highlight the imperfections of the current public–private system of health care financing and delivery and contrast these with an ideological vision of a future egalitarian [system in which people are treated equally] condition in which these imperfections will disappear and everyone will have access to "free" health care. Although the egalitarian vision holds perennial appeal for some Americans, it would impose a socialist-style command economy and require government control of the production and distribution of goods and services. The striking feature of the command economy, as Professor Alain Enthoven of Stanford University, has observed, is "the contradiction between system and pretensions on the one hand, performance on the other." Policymakers have a duty to examine not only the promises of the single-payer proposal, but also its performance.

Socialism does not work, or at least not very well, based on an ample historical record. Yet supporters of nationalized health care still believe that socialism, through single-payer financing, is uniquely capable of succeeding in the discrete area of health care financing and

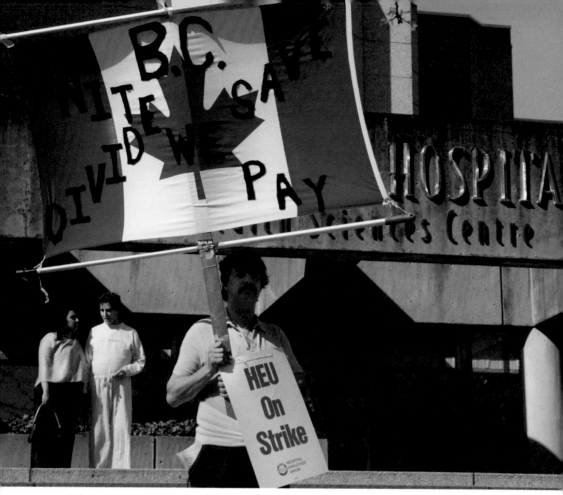

*The author points to the 2004 British Columbia health care workers' strike as an adverse effect of the single-payer system because so many needed surgeries were canceled due to the strike.*

delivery. Just as nations have learned that political management and control is not the best way to run the coal, steel, farming, banking, airline, or electric power industries, policymakers should conclude that the political process is a poor way to manage health care. Preventing human suffering should, in principle, include rejecting systems that decrease available health resources by depressing general living standards. Any health care intervention, especially any that affects large populations, should scrupulously follow the medical maxim of "first, do no harm."

## Adverse Effects

Health care in a single-payer system will be rationed by means other than price. This will have inevitable adverse effects, including:

- *Long waits and reduced quality.* In Britain, over 800,000 patients are waiting for hospital care. In Canada, the average wait between a general practitioner referral and a specialty consultation has been over 17 weeks. Beyond queuing for care or services, single-payer systems are often characterized by strict drug formularies, limited treatment options, and discrimination by age in the provision of care. Price controls, a routine feature of such systems, also result in reduced drug, technology, and medical device research.

- *Funding crises.* Because individuals remain insulated from the direct costs of health care, as in many third-party payment systems, health care appears to be "free." As a result, demand expands while government officials devise ways to control costs. The shortest route is by providing fewer products and services through explicit and implicit rationing.

- *New inequalities.* Beyond favoritism in the provision of care for the politically well-connected, single-payer health care systems often restrain costs by limiting surgeries for the elderly, restricting dialysis, withholding care from very premature infants, reducing the number of intensive care beds, limiting MRI availability, and restricting access to specialists.

> **FAST FACT**
>
> The United States has over 30 computerized tomography (CT) scanners—medical imaging devices used in diagnosis—per million people, whereas Canada has less than 15, and the United Kingdom less than 10, per million people.

- *Labor strikes and personnel shortages.* In 2004, a health worker strike in British Columbia, Canada, resulted in the cancellation of 5,300 surgeries and numerous MRI examinations, CT scans, and lab tests. Canada also has a shortage of physicians, and the recruitment and retention of doctors in Britain has become a chronic problem.

- *Outdated facilities and medical equipment.* Advances in medical technology are often seen in terms of their costs rather than their benefits, and investment is slower. For example, an estimated 60 percent of radiological equipment in Canada is technically outdated.

# Median Wait by Province in 2006: Weeks Waited from Referral by General Practitioner (GP) to Treatment

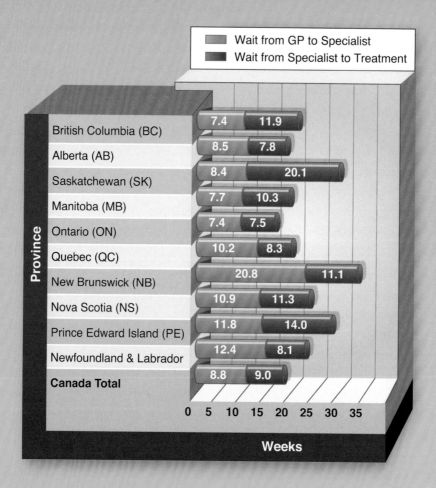

**Wait from GP to Specialist**
**Wait from Specialist to Treatment**

| Province | Wait from GP to Specialist | Wait from Specialist to Treatment |
|---|---|---|
| British Columbia (BC) | 7.4 | 11.9 |
| Alberta (AB) | 8.5 | 7.8 |
| Saskatchewan (SK) | 8.4 | 20.1 |
| Manitoba (MB) | 7.7 | 10.3 |
| Ontario (ON) | 7.4 | 7.5 |
| Quebec (QC) | 10.2 | 8.3 |
| New Brunswick (NB) | 20.8 | 11.1 |
| Nova Scotia (NS) | 10.9 | 11.3 |
| Prince Edward Island (PE) | 11.8 | 14.0 |
| Newfoundland & Labrador | 12.4 | 8.1 |
| **Canada Total** | 8.8 | 9.0 |

Weeks: 0 5 10 15 20 25 30 35

Taken from: The Fraser Institute's national waiting list survey. "Waiting Your Turn," 16th edition, 2006.

- *Politicization and lost liberty.* Patient autonomy is curtailed in favor of the judgment of an elite few, who dictate what health care needs and desires *ought* to be while imposing social controls over activities deemed undesirable or at odds with an expanding definition of "public health." Government officials would claim a compelling interest in many areas now considered personal.

## The Market Approach

The very real problems of America's health care system, including the problem of uninsurance, can be addressed through innovative market-based solutions. While critics of the market approach are free to claim that a future health care system based on free and voluntary exchange would have pernicious [destructive] rather than positive effects, the evidence-based approach to health policy finds little to support the promised superiority of national health insurance. In the end, the socialist vision of medicine will achieve Orwellian [referring to situations George Orwell described as being detrimental to a free society] results: The promise of health care coverage becomes health rationing, access to universal coverage means delays in access to care, official fairness yields to favoritism by officials, freedom of choice becomes coerced conformity, and democratic deliberation is replaced by bureaucratic decision-making.

**EVALUATING THE AUTHOR'S ARGUMENTS:**

In this viewpoint Fleming argues that no evidence points to the superiority of a single-payer health care system over other systems, and he raises several concerns about the system. At issue in this viewpoint—and throughout this chapter—is a debate about how to weigh the competing values of universal coverage, individual choice, affordability, and quality. Rank each viewpoint in this chapter according to these values. Which viewpoint do you think is superior overall?

# Facts About Health Care

Editor's note: These facts can be used in reports or papers to reinforce or add credibility when making important points or claims.

## Types of Health Care

- *Private.* Health care paid for by private health insurance, with care through private doctors and hospitals.
- *Public.* Health care paid for by public, or government, funds, with care through either private or public doctors and hospitals.
- *Consumer-Driven.* Health care decisions made mainly by consumers and less by insurers, employers, and government.
- *Single-Payer.* All health care paid for by the government through taxes collected, offering care through a public health care network or by providing vouchers for private care.
- *Universal.* All people have health care, either through a government-sponsored single-payer plan or through mandated—and sometimes subsidized—health insurance.

## Types of U.S. Government–Sponsored Health Insurance

- *Medicare.* A health insurance program for people aged sixty-five or older, people under age sixty-five with certain disabilities, and people of all ages with end-stage renal disease (permanent kidney failure requiring dialysis or a kidney transplant).
- *Medicaid.* A joint federal and state program that helps with medical costs for some people with low incomes and limited resources; each state sets its own guidelines regarding eligibility and services.
- *Military.* Includes CHAMPUS (Comprehensive Health and Medical Plan for Uniformed Services)/Tricare and CHAMPVA (Civilian Health and Medical Program of the Department of Veterans Affairs), as well as care provided by the Department of Veterans Affairs and the military.
- *State Children's Health Insurance Program (SCHIP).* A federal program that gives matching funds to states in order to provide health insurance to families with children who do not qualify for Medicaid.

## Health Insurance

According to the U.S. Census Bureau, in 2007:

- 45.7 million people—15.3 percent of the population—did not have health insurance, including 8.1 million children under eighteen years old.
- 12.7 percent of native-born American residents were uninsured and 33.2 percent of foreign-born residents were uninsured, but among foreign-born naturalized citizens only 17.6 percent were uninsured.
- 10.4 percent of the non-Hispanic white population, 32.1 percent of Hispanics, and 19.5 percent of the black population were uninsured.
- 24.5 percent of people in households with annual incomes of less than $25,000 had no health insurance coverage, whereas 7.8 percent of people in households with incomes of $75,000 or more were uninsured.
- 253.4 million people had health insurance, with 202 million covered by private health insurance and 83 million covered by government health insurance (some had both).
- 13.2 percent of the population was on Medicaid and 13.8 percent on Medicare.
- 59.3 percent of people were covered by employment-based health insurance.

## U.S. Life Expectancy and Infant Mortality

According to the U.S. Centers for Disease Control and Prevention (CDC), in 2005:

- The life expectancy at birth was 77.8 years for the entire population, with a life expectancy of 80.4 for females and 75.2 years for males.
- The life expectancy for blacks was 73.2 years, whereas the life expectancy for whites was 78.3 years.
- The top three leading causes of death were heart disease, cancer, and stroke.
- The infant mortality rate was 6.87 infant deaths per 1,000 live births.

## Global Life Expectancy and Infant Mortality

According to Central Intelligence Agency (CIA) *World Factbook* estimates, in 2009:

- The five countries with the highest life expectancy at birth are Macau (84.4 years), Andorra (82.5), Japan (82.1), Singapore (82.0), and San Marino (82.0).

- The five countries with the lowest life expectancy at birth are Swaziland (31.9 years), Angola (38.2 years), Zambia (38.6 years), Lesotho (40.4 years), and Mozambique (41.2 years).
- The United States ranked fiftieth in life expectancy out of 225 countries.

## Per Thousand Live Births:
- The five countries with the highest infant mortality were Angola (180.2), Sierra Leone (154.4), Afghanistan (152.0), Liberia (138.2), and Niger (116.7).
- The five countries with the lowest infant mortality were Singapore (2.3), Bermuda (2.5), Sweden (2.8), Japan (2.8), and Hong Kong (2.9).
- In a ranking of infant mortality from lowest to highest, the United States ranked forty-sixth out of 224 countries.

# Organizations to Contact

The editors have compiled the following list of organizations concerned with the issues debated in this book. The descriptions are derived from materials provided by the organizations. All have publications or information available for interested readers. The list was compiled on the date of publication of the present volume; the information provided here may change. Be aware that many organizations take several weeks or longer to respond to queries, so allow as much time as possible.

**Alliance for Health Reform**
1444 I St. NW, Ste. 910, Washington, DC 20005-6573
(202) 789-2300
e-mail: info@allhealth.org
Web site: www.allhealth.org

The Alliance for Health Reform exists to provide unbiased information to understand the roots of the nation's health care problems and the trade-offs posed by competing proposals for change. The Alliance for Health Reform believes that everyone in the United States should have health coverage at a reasonable cost, but rather than taking positions on legislation, the organization focuses its efforts on holding informational forums. The Alliance for Health Reform produces issue briefs regularly on topics such as "Covering the Uninsured: Options for Reform" and "How Wide Has the Window Opened for Health Reform?"

**Alliance to Defend Health Care**
1534 Tremont St., Boston, MA 02120
(617) 784-6367
e-mail: contact@defendhealth.org
Web site: www.massdefendhealthcare.org

The Alliance to Defend Health Care is a group of health care professionals and others who believe that health care is a fundamental human right and that the delivery of health care should be guided by science and compassion, not by corporate self-interest. The alliance collaborates with others to foster a broad public dialogue and health policy reforms to achieve universal access to high-quality, affordable health care for all. The Alliance to Defend Health Care has several resources available at their Web site, including "Principles of Health Care Delivery and Practice."

**American Enterprise Institute for Public Policy Research (AEI)**
1150 Seventeenth St. NW, Washington, DC 20036
(202) 862-5800
e-mail: info@aei.org
Web site: www.aei.org

The American Enterprise Institute for Public Policy Research (AEI) is a private, nonpartisan, nonprofit institution dedicated to research and education on issues of government, politics, economics, and social welfare. AEI sponsors research and publishes materials that encourage defending the principles and improving the institutions of American freedom and democratic capitalism. Among AEI's publications is the book *Innovation and Technology Adoption in Health Care Markets.*

**Campaign for an American Solution**
601 Pennsylvania Ave. NW, South Building, Ste. 500
Washington, DC 20004
(202) 778-3200
e-mail: info@americanhealthsolution.org
Web site: www.americanhealthsolution.org

The Campaign for an American Solution is sponsored by America's Health Insurance Plans (AHIP), the national trade association for health insurance companies. The mission of the campaign is to build support for workable health care reform based on core principles supported by the American people, and it works to facilitate a constructive conversation to that end. The campaign has published a health care proposal, "Now Is the Time for Health Care Reform: A Proposal to Achieve Universal Coverage, Affordability, Quality Improvement, and Market Reform," available at the campaign's Web site.

**Cato Institute**
1000 Massachusetts Ave. NW, Washington, DC 20001
(202) 842-0200
Web site: www.cato.org

The Cato Institute is a public policy research foundation dedicated to limiting the role of government, protecting individual liberties, and promoting free markets. Cato has been a longtime advocate of deregulating the health care industry so that consumers can afford the health care insurance and treatment of their choice. Among the institute's publications is the book *Healthy Competition: What's Holding Back Health Care and How to Free It.*

**The Commonwealth Fund**
1 East 75th St., New York, NY 10021
(212) 606-3800
e-mail: info@cmwf.org
Web site: www.commonwealthfund.org

The Commonwealth Fund is a private foundation that aims to promote a high-performing health care system that achieves better access, improved quality, and greater efficiency, particularly for society's most vulnerable, including low-income people, the uninsured, minority Americans, young children, and elderly adults. The fund carries out this mandate by supporting independent research on health care issues and making grants to improve health care practice and policy. The foundation publishes an annual report and *The Commonwealth Fund Digest,* both of which are available at the Web site.

**Georgetown Health Policy Institute**
Georgetown University, 3300
Whitehaven St. NW, Ste. 5000, Box 571444, Washington, DC 20057
(202) 687-0880
Web site: ihcrp.georgetown.edu

The Georgetown Health Policy Institute is a multidisciplinary group of faculty and staff dedicated to conducting research on key issues in health policy and health services research. Institute members are engaged in a wide diversity of projects, focusing on issues relating to health care financing, the uninsured, federal health insurance reforms, quality of care and outcomes research, mental health services research, and the impact of changes in the health care market on providers and patients. Publications sponsored by the institute include "Medicaid and State Budgets: Looking at the Facts."

**Health Care for America NOW! (HCAN)**
1825 K St. NW, Ste. 400, Washington, DC 20006
(202) 454-6200
e-mail: info@healthcareforamericanow.org
Web site: www.healthcareforamericanow.org

HCAN is a national grassroots campaign of more than 850 organizations in 46 states representing 30 million people dedicated to winning quality, affordable health care. HCAN works to mobilize people in their communities to lobby their U.S. senators and representatives in Congress to stand up to the insurance companies and other special interest groups to achieve quality, affordable health care. Among the publications available at HCAN's Web site is their "Statement of Common Purpose," explaining the proposed reform of the U.S. health care system.

**Healthcare—NOW!**
339 Lafayette St., New York, NY 10012
(800) 453-1305
e-mail: info@healthcare-now.org
Web site: www.healthcare-now.org

Healthcare—NOW! is an education and advocacy organization that addresses the health insurance crisis in the United States. Healthcare—NOW! advocates for the passage of national, single-payer health care legislation, specifically campaigning for the National Health Care Act, HR 676. Available at the organization's Web site is the full text of the proposed legislation.

**Heartland Institute**
19 South LaSalle St., #903, Chicago, IL 60603
(312) 377-4000
e-mail: publications@heartland.org
Web site: www.heartland.org

The mission of the Heartland Institute is to discover and promote free-market solutions to social and economic problems. The institute's Health Care Policy Issue Suite is a comprehensive resource for people who support a free-market approach to improving the nation's health care system. The institute publishes *Consumer Power Report* and *Health Care News*, their national outreach publications for the consumer-driven health care movement; *Heartland Policy Studies*, peer-reviewed original research on health care topics; and *Research & Commentaries*, collections of the best available research on hot topics in the health care reform debate.

**Physicians for a National Health Program (PNHP)**
29 E. Madison, Ste. 602, Chicago, IL 60602
(312) 782-6006
e-mail: info@pnhp.org
Web site: www.pnhp.org

PNHP is a nonprofit research and education organization of sixteen thousand physicians, medical students, and health professionals who support single-payer national health insurance. PNHP performs research on the need for fundamental health care system reform, coordinates speakers and forums, participates in town hall meetings and debates, contributes scholarly articles to peer-reviewed medical journals, and appears regularly on national television and news programs advocating for a single-payer system. Among the research papers sponsored by PNHP is "Illness and Injury as Contributors to Bankruptcy."

**Urban Institute**
2100 M St. NW, Washington, DC 20037
(202) 833-7200
Web site: www.urban.org

The Urban Institute works to foster sound public policy and effective government by gathering data, conducting research, evaluating programs, offering technical assistance overseas, and educating Americans on social and economic issues. The institute's Health Policy Center analyzes trends and underlying causes of changes in health insurance coverage, access to care, and use of health care services by the entire U.S. population. The Urban Institute publishes a variety of resources, including books such as *Health Policy and the Uninsured*.

# For Further Reading

## Books

Barlett, Donald L., and James B. Steele. *Critical Condition: How Health Care in America Became Big Business—and Bad Medicine.* New York: Broadway, 2005. Profiles patients and doctors seemingly trapped by the health care system, in the process illuminating pitfalls of the system overall.

Brownlee, Shannon. *Overtreated: Why Too Much Medicine Is Making Us Sicker and Poorer.* New York: Bloomsbury, 2007. Debunks the idea that most of medicine is based on sound science and shows how the health care system delivers huge amounts of unnecessary care that is not only wasteful but can actually imperil the health of patients.

Cannon, Michael F., and Michael D. Tanner. *Healthy Competition: What's Holding Back Health Care and How to Free It.* Washington, DC: Cato Institute, 2007. Analyzes the best and worst ideas in health care reform—on both the right and the left—concluding that removing government restrictions will result in higher quality and lower prices.

Cogan, John F., R. Glenn Hubbard, and Daniel P. Kessler. *Healthy, Wealthy, and Wise: Five Steps to a Better Health Care System.* Washington, DC: AEI, 2005. Proposes five key policies to build a better health-care system: (1) health care tax reform, (2) insurance reform, (3) improvement of health care information, (4) control of anticompetitive behavior, and (5) malpractice system reform.

Cohn, Jonathan. *Sick: The Untold Story of America's Health Care Crisis—and the People Who Pay the Price.* New York: HarperPerennial, 2008. Interweaves tragic stories of ordinary Americans with reporting from Washington, chronicling the decline of America's health care system.

Daschle, Tom, with Scott S. Greenberger and Jeanne M. Lambrew. *Critical: What We Can Do About the Health-Care Crisis.* New York: Thomas Dunne, 2008. Offers solutions to the problems of the U.S. health care system and creates a blueprint for solving the crisis.

Emanuel, Ezekiel J. *Healthcare, Guaranteed: A Simple, Secure Solution for America.* Jackson, TN: PublicAffairs, 2008. Offers a plan to comprehensively restructure the delivery and quality of health care, eliminating employer health care and establishing an independent program to evaluate health care plans and insurance companies.

Garson, Arthur, Jr., and Carolyn L. Engelhard. *Health Care Half-Truths: Too Many Myths, Not Enough Reality.* Lanham, MD: Rowman & Littlefield, 2007. Untangles the misinformation, misperceptions, and confusion about the U.S. health care system that have confounded the American public and elected officials.

Gratzer, David. *The Cure: How Capitalism Can Save American Health Care.* New York: Encounter, 2008. Argues that the crisis in American health care stems largely from its addiction to outmoded and discredited economic ideas.

Herzlinger, Regina E. *Who Killed Health Care? America's $2 Trillion Medical Problem—and the Consumer-Driven Cure.* New York: McGraw-Hill, 2007. Exposes the motives and methods of those who have crippled America's health care system, including figures in the insurance, hospital, employment, governmental, and academic sectors.

Jonas, Steven, Raymond Goldsteen, and Karen Goldsteen. *Introduction to the U.S. Health Care System.* New York: Springer, 2007. Provides an accessible overview of the basic components of the system: health care personnel, hospitals and other institutions, the federal government, financing and payment mechanisms, and managed care.

Kling, Arnold. *Crisis of Abundance: Rethinking How We Pay for Health Care.* Washington, DC: Cato Institute, 2006. Argues that the way we finance health care matches neither the needs of patients nor the way medicine is practiced, and proposes a solution.

Longman, Phillip. *Best Care Anywhere: Why VA Health Care Is Better than Yours.* Polipoint, 2007. Uses the Veterans Health Administration turnaround to illustrate lessons for the U.S. health care system.

Porter, Michael E., and Elizabeth Olmsted Teisberg. *Redefining Health Care: Creating Value-Based Competition on Results.*

Cambridge, MA: Harvard Business School Press, 2006. Argues that participants in the health care system have competed to shift costs, accumulate bargaining power, and restrict services rather than create value for patients, recommending movement to a positive-sum competition.

Relman, Arnold. *A Second Opinion: Rescuing America's Health Care.* Jackson, TN: PublicAffairs, 2007. Traces the rise of the current health care system, arguing for significant changes to the current system, with all health care facilities operating as nonprofit entities.

Rooney, J. Patrick, and Dan Perrin. *America's Health Care Crisis Solved: Money-Saving Solutions, Coverage for Everyone.* Indianapolis, IN: Wiley, 2008. Highlights the major pitfalls of our current health care system and shows why, without changes, health care costs will soon demolish the American economy as well as the opportunity to receive quality care.

## Periodicals

Antos, Joseph, and Alice M. Rivlin. "Slowing the Rising Costs of Health Care Possible," *Times-Union* (Albany, NY), April 4, 2007.

Bailey, Ronald. "Your Money or Your Life: Medical Spending Still a Good Value," *Reason Online*, September 15, 2006.

Beane, Billy, Newt Gingrich, and John Kerry. "How to Take American Health Care from Worst to First," *New York Times*, October 24, 2008.

Boodman, Sandra G. "Seeing Red: The Rising Costs of Care and a Failing Economy Drive More Americans into Medical Debt," *Washington Post*, January 13, 2009.

Boudreaux, Donald J. "The Way to Better, Cheaper Healthcare: Don't Make It a Human Right," *Christian Science Monitor*, October 17, 2006.

Broder, David. "For a Change, Movement on Health Care Reform," *Record* (Bergen County, NJ), November 29, 2008.

Burger, Deborah. "On Health Care Reform: Long Waits Are Really Sicko," *San Francisco Chronicle*, July 10, 2007.

Cape, Keven. "French Health Care Problematic in U.S.," *Register-Guard* (Eugene, OR), August 19, 2007.

*Christianity Today.* "The Health Care Crunch: Let's Make Sure Any Reform Plan We Pursue Avoids the Single-Value Syndrome," February 2008.

Crighton, K. Andrew. "Chronic Diseases Drive Health Care Costs," *Record* (Bergen County, NJ), July 8, 2008.

Dalrymple, Theodore. "Health of the State: Doctors, Patients, and Michael Moore," *National Review*, August 13, 2007.

DeMoro, Rose Ann. "Obama and Daschle Should Opt for Single-Payer," *Progressive*, December 11, 2008.

Freudenheim, Milt. "With Health Care Topic A, Some Sketches for a Solution," *New York Times*, January 25, 2007.

Furnas, Ben. "American Health Care Since 1994: The Unacceptable Status Quo," Center for American Progress, January 8, 2009.

Garson, Arthur, Jr. "Healthcare's Wasted Billions," *Christian Science Monitor*, October 8, 2008.

Gawande, Atul. "Sick and Twisted," *New Yorker*, July 23, 2007.

Gingrich, Newt, and Sheldon Whitehouse. "Next President Must Put Health in Health Care," *Washington Times*, October 28, 2008.

Glusker, Peter. "Universal Health Care That's Not-for-Profit Can Work," *National Catholic Reporter*, September 21, 2007.

Goodman, Amy. "Nothing to Fear but No Health Care," *Seattle Times*, January 16, 2009.

Gottlieb, Scott. "What Medicaid Tells Us About Government Health Care," *Wall Street Journal*, January 8, 2009.

Herdt, Timm. "Put Healthcare at the Top," *Ventura County Star*, January 14, 2009.

Herzlinger, Regina. "America, Insure Thyself," *Washington Post*, March 29, 2008.

Hsieh, Paul. "Universal Healthcare and the Waistline Police," *Christian Science Monitor*, January 7, 2009.

Hutchison, Sue. "Health Care Reform Needed to Keep Saving Lives Like These," *San Jose Mercury News*, February 5, 2008.

Iverson, David, and Elinor Christiansen. "Single-Payer Health Care Is Way to Go," *Rocky Mountain News*, September 4, 2006.

Kemble, Stephen. "For Healthcare, Single-Payer System Is Best," *Honolulu Advertiser*, January 23, 2009.

Kinsley, Michael. "To Your Health: Why Modest Reform Is Preferable to Single-Payer Health Care," *Slate*, March 17, 2006. www.slate.com.

Laurant, Darrell. "Is Health Care Really That Bad?" *News & Advance* (Lynchburg VA), November 24, 2008.

Layton, Mary Jo. "Ripping Off Dr. America," *Record* (Bergen County, NJ), June 10, 2007.

McCanne, Don. "Disputations: Is Single-Payer Health Care the Best Option?" *New Republic*, July 16, 2008.

McCaughey, Betsy. "The Truth About Mandatory Health Insurance," *Wall Street Journal*, January 4, 2008.

Morris, Charles R. "Health Care for All: Not Easy, Not Cheap, but Possible," *Commonweal*, August 15, 2008.

Morrison, Patt. "Insurance Is Enough to Make You Sick; Private Health Insurance Is a Drag on the Economy the Government Must Fix," *Los Angeles Times*, January 4, 2007.

*New York Times*. "The High Cost of Health Care," November 25, 2007.

Noah, Timothy. "Time to Socialize Medicine," *Slate*, November 8, 2006.

Peikoff, Leonard. "Health Insurance Is Not a 'Right,'" FrontPage Magazine.com, January 18, 2007. www.frontpagemagazine.com.

Price, Tom. "Transforming Health Care: Provide Access and Ownership to Patients First," *Washington Times*, July 31, 2008.

Proffitt, Waldo. "HMOs a Model? Hardly," *Sarasota Herald Tribune*, October 8, 2006.

Quinn, Bryant. "We Can Afford Universal Health Care," *Newsweek*, July 30, 2007.

*Register-Guard* (Eugene, OR). "The Best Health Care Plan," March 2, 2008.

Riley, Kate. "Nibbling at the Edges of Health Care," *Seattle Times*, January 21, 2008.

Schoonmaker, Mary Ellen. "Wrong Place, Wrong Time for Universal Health Care," *Record* (Bergen County, NJ), March 27, 2008.

Schorr, Daniel. "America's Struggle with Health Care," *Record* (Bergen County, NJ), February 4, 2007.

Seate, Mike. "Time Has Arrived for Universal Health Care," *Pittsburgh Tribune-Review*, March 4, 2008.

Smith, Richard. "Everyone Could Be a Winner," *Guardian* (UK), November 6, 2006.

Terry, Ken. "On Health Care Reform: For Employers, There's No Exit from Health Care," *San Francisco Chronicle*, July 10, 2007.

Weintraub, Daniel. "Sales Tax for Health Care Plan Poses a Dilemma," *Sacramento Bee*, September 16, 2007.

Williams, Ronald. "A System Where No American Is Denied Healthcare," *Financial Times*, October 27, 2008.

# Index